DEC   2014

Quick
Icelandic Knits

Gunn
Birgirsdottir

T|S
TRAFALGAR SQUARE
North Pomfret, Vermont

First published in the United States of America
in 2014 by
Trafalgar Square Books
North Pomfret, Vermont 05053

Originally published in Norwegian as *Gøy å strikke med tykke pinner*

© Cappelen Damm AS, 2010
© J. W. Cappelen Forlag as
English translation © 2014 Trafalgar Square Books

ISBN: 978-1-57076-581-0

Library of Congress Control Number: 2013937969

Translation by Carol Huebscher Rhoades
Photography: Gunn Birgirsdottir
Graphic Design: unniform as
Reproduction: Capella Media

Printed in China

TABLE OF CONTENTS

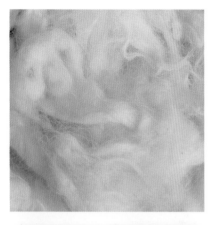

FOREWORD

I knitted my first sweater when I was 9 years old. I found an old pattern for a Fana sweater and used leftover yarns from my mother's many knitting projects. It was a very colorful sweater and you can imagine how proud I was to have created my own garment. I left the finishing to my mother—and that's how I continued for many years, before I dared doing it myself. When I began knitting garments in the round, finishing was so much easier. With circular knitting and raglan shaping you only have to seam the underarms.

There is hardly a day when I don't knit, and I like it that way. Even before finishing one project, I'm already planning the next. Knitting offers endless possibilities. It is exciting to arrange the colors and make new variations of the models. Just by changing the colors, the ribbing, or the neck, you can make your own favorite garment starting from a basic pattern. Some people like sweaters with a high neckline or turtleneck, others prefer a short neck; some like long garments and others like short ones.

Before you begin knitting, it's a good idea to choose the colors for your garment. Sometimes you like the colors but not the design or maybe you like the design but not the colors. These are easy problems to solve and that is exactly what I want to show you how to do in this book.

I want this book to inspire you with ideas instead of being just a pattern book.

Play with colors—be creative and knit your own favorite garments.

Good luck!

Gunn Birgirsdottir

YARN INFORMATION

Álafoss Lopi: 100% wool, 100 g (3.5 oz) approx. 109 yd / 100 m was used.

If you are unable to obtain any of the yarn used in this book, it can be replaced with a yarn of a similar weight and composition. Please note, however, the finished projects may vary slightly from those shown, depending on the yarn used.

For more information on selecting or substituting yarn contact your local yarn shop or an online store, they are familiar with all types of yarns and would be happy to help you. Additionally, the online knitting community at Ravelry.com has forums where you can post questions about specific yarns. Yarns come and go so quickly and there are so many beautiful yarns available.

HISTORY OF ICELANDIC WOOL

I've knitted all the models in this book with Icelandic wool (Álafoss Lopi) but you can certainly substitute another similar wool yarn. Each pattern lists the gauge and amount of yarn.

Vikings arrived in Iceland in AD 874 and brought two kinds of domesticated animals with them. Icelandic horses and Icelandic sheep are both unique examples of their breeds. Over the course of time, they have had as much significance for the history of our country as the people who settled it. From the very beginning, Icelanders have had a hard fight for existence against merciless natural forces. Horses were important for transportation and work while sheep were the key to survival for the entire country. Sheep meat has been an important source of sustenance for generations of Icelanders and wool gave protection against the harsh Icelandic climate.

Medieval saga writers were inspired by heroic deeds and elegant writing but they also discussed daily life and work on farms, such as sheep shearing, carding, spinning, and knitting, which are very old traditions that have changed very little over the years.

As a sheep breed, Icelandic sheep are very special. The purity of the breed has been preserved through centuries of isolation and, due to this isolation, the wool is also very special. It is one of the warmest wools in the world.

Over the course of 1,100 winters, the fleeces of Icelandic sheep have proven durable against the hard subarctic climate of the island. The fleece has two types of fiber: the long and smooth outer coat of hair, which is strong and water resistant; and the soft, fine mohair-like inner coat, which very effectively insulates against the cold.

In a time of increasing interest in the environment, it is important to emphasize that Icelandic wool products are environmentally friendly, developed as they have been in the centuries-long interaction between humans and nature. Only natural energy sources such as water power and geothermal heat are used to process the wool. The sheep that the wool comes from spend most of their lives on the mountains in undisturbed nature. Only the finest wool becomes yarn. The raw wool is purchased from farmers and then sorted by wool experts and sent on for washing at local processors throughout the island.

The wool is cleaned with the smallest possible amount of washing soap and chemical treatment. As much as possible, the natural oils are retained in the wool fibers so that the wool maintains the warmth, lightness, and water-repellent qualities that nature has endowed it with. Then, and only then, the finest quality wool is selected for spinning into beautiful yarn that can be further processed into a broad spectrum of knitted products.

Durable but also soft, tough but also comfortable—that defines Icelandic wool products.

KNITTING IN THE ROUND

Knitting in the round is one of several knitting techniques. Personally I am very happy to knit in the round because it is easy knitting and requires little finishing. The only seaming you have to do is at the underarms. The body and sleeves are each knitted in the round on circular needles up to the underarm. The pieces are then joined on one circular and the yoke is knit in the round.

On the following pages you'll find 7 models for knitting in the round.

Most people start by choosing the colors when planning a knitted garment. Sometimes you like the colors but not the design or maybe you like the design but not the colors. These are easy problems to solve and that is exactly what I want to show you how to do with this book. As a starting point, I've chosen one basic pattern and made 7 variations on it. These variations can also be used for other models described in this book.

1 Knit the body and one sleeve up to the underarm. Bind off for the underarm and armhole on the body (see basic pattern).

2 Knit the 1st sleeve onto the same needle as for the body.

6

3 Knit the 2nd sleeve the same way and knit it onto the same needle as for the body.

4 Knit around in your chosen pattern and work the decreases following the chart.

Three-needle bind-off to knit the underarm seams together

(the stitches that are placed on waste yarn or stitch holder for the underarm)

Turn the piece inside out so that the wrong side (WS) faces outwards. Divide the stitches from the holders evenly onto two needles. Hold the needles parallel to each other and, with a third needle, knit the first st on each needle together, *knit the first st on each needle together and bind off. Repeat from * until all the sts have been bound off. Use duplicate stitch to join the little opening left at each end of the underarm seam.

Joining the underarm seam with duplicate stitch

(when the stitches have been previously bound off)

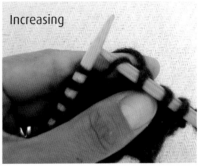

Increasing

Techniques

Increasing and decreasing stitches

To increase one stitch (M1), insert the needle under the strand between 2 stitches, twist it as you place it on the left needle, and knit into it (through back loop).

To decrease 1 stitch, knit 2 stitches together (k2tog). Insert the right needle knitwise into the 2nd st from the end of the left needle and then into the first st; bring yarn around the needle and through the two stitches to knit them together; slip sts from the needle.

Decreasing

Needles

Circular U.S. size 7 / 4.5 mm (24-32 in / 60-80 cm) for the ribbing.
Circular U.S. size 10 / 6 mm (24-32 in / 60-80 cm) for the body.
Circular U.S. size 10 / 6 mm (16 in / 40 cm) for the sleeves and smaller garments such as hats, bags, and slippers, etc.
Double-pointed needles (dpn) U.S. size 7 / 4.5 mm for ribbing on the sleeves.
Double-pointed needles U.S. size 10 / 6 mm for the sleeves (when the stitch count is too small to fit around a circular needle) and for finishing smaller garments.

You need at least 40 stitches for working around on a 16 in / 40 cm long circular needle.

Ribbing can also be worked on a circular U.S. size 7 / 4.5 mm (24-32 in / 60-80 cm) by working back and forth and then seaming afterwards.

Casting on

1 Hold a needle in your right hand. Pull out some yarn from the ball (about 3 yd/m for a child's size and 3½ yd/m for adult sizes). At the center of the long strand, make a slip knot with the yarn (as when working finger crochet). Place the loop on the needle.

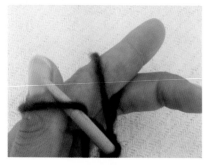

2 Lay one strand over your left thumb—from the back of the thumb and forward—and the other strand over your left index finger. Hold the strands a little loosely.

3 Insert the needle through the loop on the thumb.

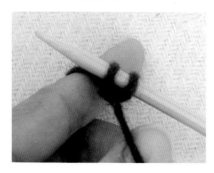

4 Catch the strand over the index finger and bring that strand through the loop.

5 Tighten carefully.

Abbreviations

beg	begin, beginning
BO	bind off (= British cast off)
CC	contrast color
ch	chain
cm	centimeter(s)
CO	cast on
dec	decrease
dpn	double-pointed needles
g	gram(s)
in	inch(es)
inc	increase
k	knit
k2tog	knit 2 together (right-leaning decrease)
M1	make 1 = lift strand between two sts and knit into back loop
MC	main color
m	meter(s)
mm	millimeter(s)
p	purl
rnd(s)	round(s)
RS	right side
sc	single crochet (= British double crochet)
sl	slip
ssk	(slip 1 knitwise) 2 times, insert left needle into back of the 2 sts and knit together (left-leaning decrease, substitutes for sl 1, k1, psso)
st(s)	stitch(es)
tbl	through back loop
WS	wrong side
wyb	with yarn held in back of work
yd	yards
yo	yarnover
Stockinette = British stocking st (knit on RS and purl on WS)	

Basic Pattern for Children's Sweaters

Sizes: 5 (7, 9, 10, 12) years
Chest: 30¾ (32¾, 34¾, 36¼, 38¼) in / 78 (83, 88, 92, 97) cm
Length from neck at center front:
16½ (18¼, 19¾, 21¼, 22¾) in / 42 (46, 50, 54, 58) cm
Sleeve length: 9¾ (11½, 13, 13¾, 15) in / 25 (29, 33, 35, 38) cm
Gauge: 13 sts and 18 rnds on needles U.S. size 10 /
6 mm = 4 x 4 in / 10 x 10 cm
Yarn: CYCA #5, 100 g = 109 yd / 100 m

Body
With your choice of yarn color and smaller size circular, CO 92 (96, 102, 108, 112) sts; join, being careful not to twist cast-on row. Work around in k1, p1 rib for 2 (2, 2, 2, 2½) in / 5 (5, 5, 5, 6) cm or desired length (see pages 14, 15, and 24). On the next rnd, inc 10 (12, 12, 12, 14) sts evenly spaced around = 102 (108, 114, 120, 126) sts total. Change to larger size circular and work in desired pattern. Continue in stockinette until piece measures 9¾ (11, 11¾, 13, 14¼) in / 25 (28, 30, 33, 36) cm but do *not* knit the last 4 (4, 5, 4, 4) sts on the last rnd. Do *not* cut yarn.

Sleeves
With your choice of yarn color and smaller size dpn, CO 24 (24, 26, 26, 28) sts; join, being careful not to twist cast-on row. Work k1, p1 rib as for bottom of sweater body and then increase 12 (12, 10, 10, 14) sts evenly spaced around on the last round for a total of 36 (36, 36, 36, 42) sts. Change to larger size circular and continue around in stockinette. Work in a pattern if you like. *At the same time,* increase 1 st at the beg and 1 st at the end of every 6th rnd 4 (5, 6, 7, 5) times = a total of 44 (46, 48, 50, 52) sts. Continue without further shaping until sleeve is 9¾ (11½, 13, 13¾, 15) in / 25 (29, 33, 35, 38) cm long.
Place the last 5 (4, 5, 5, 4) and the first 4 (4, 4, 4, 4) sts on a holder. Make the other sleeve the same way.

Yoke
Join the sleeves and body as follows: Place the last 4 (4, 5, 4, 4) and the first 4 (4, 4, 4, 4) sts of the round on the body onto waste yarn or a stitch holder. With the larger size circular and your choice of yarn color, k35 (38, 39, 41, 44) sts of sleeve #1, k43 (45, 47, 51, 55) sts of the front; place the next 8 (8, 9, 8, 8) sts on a holder; 35 (38, 39, 41, 44) sts of sleeve #2, k43 (47, 49, 53, 55) sts of the back = a total of 156 (168, 174, 186, 198) sts.

Choose your color pattern and shape the yoke as shown on the chart (change to dpn when the sts no longer fit around the circular). After completing charted rows, 52 (56, 58, 62, 66) sts remain.

Neckband
With smaller size dpn, knit 1 rnd in desired color and, *at the same time,* decrease 2 (6, 8, 10, 14) sts evenly spaced around = a total of 50 (50, 50, 52, 52) sts remain. Work around in k1, p1 rib for 2¾-3¼ in / 7-8 cm and then bind off loosely. For other neckband options, see pages 14, 15, and 17.

Finishing
Weave in all ends neatly on WS. Seam the underarms with Kitchener stitch or three-needle bind-off (see page 8).

Fold down the doubled neckband to the WS and loosely sew the edge along neckline.

Basic Pattern for Adult Sweaters

Sizes: XS (S, M, L, XL)

Chest: 40¼ (41¾, 43¾, 45¼, 47¼) in / 102 (106, 111, 115, 120) cm

Length from neck at center front:

        24½ (25½, 26¾, 27½, 28¼) in / 62 (65, 68, 70, 72) cm

Sleeve length, men's:

        18¼ (19, 19, 19¾, 19¾) in / 46 (48, 48, 50, 50) cm

Sleeve length, women's:

        16¼ (17, 17, 17¾, 17¾) in / 41 (43, 43, 45, 45) cm

Gauge: 13 sts and 18 rnds on larger needles = 4 x 4 in / 10 x 10 cm

Yarn: CYCA #5, 100 g = 109 yd / 100 m

Body

With your choice of yarn color and smaller size circular, CO 118 (124, 130, 136, 140) sts; join, being careful not to twist cast-on row. Work around in k1, p1 rib for 2½ (2½, 2½, 2½, 2¾) in / 6 (6, 6, 7, 7) cm or desired length (see pages 14, 15, and 24). On the next rnd, inc 14 (14, 14, 14, 16) sts evenly spaced around = 132 (138, 144, 150, 156) sts total. Change to larger size circular and work in desired pattern. Continue in stockinette until piece measures 15 (15¾, 16½, 17, 17¼ in / 38 (40, 42, 43, 44) cm but do not knit the last 5 (5, 6, 5, 6) sts on the last rnd. Do *not* cut yarn.

Sleeves

With your choice of yarn color and smaller size dpn, CO 28 (30, 30, 32, 32) sts; join, being careful not to twist cast-on row. Work k1, p1 rib as for bottom of sweater body and then increase 14 (12, 12, 16, 16) sts evenly spaced around on the last round for a total of 42 (42, 42, 48, 48) sts. Change to larger size dpn or circular and continue around in stockinette. Work in a pattern if you like. *At the same time,* increase 1 st at the beg and 1 st at the end of every 7th rnd 6 (7, 8, 7, 8) times for women's sizes and on every 8th rnd 6 (7, 8, 7, 8) times for men's sizes = a total of 54 (56, 58, 62, 64) sts. Continue without further shaping until sleeve is 16¼ (17, 17, 17¾, 17¾) in / 41 (43, 43, 45, 45) cm long for women's sizes and 18¼ (19, 19, 19¾, 19¾) in / 46 (48, 48, 50, 50) cm for men's sizes. Place the last 5 (5, 6, 5, 6) and the first 4 (5, 5, 5, 5) sts on a holder. Make the other sleeve the same way.

Yoke

Join the sleeves and body as follows: Place the last 5 (5, 6, 5, 6) and the first 4 (5, 5, 5, 5) sts of the round on the body onto waste yarn or a stitch holder. With the larger size circular and your choice of yarn color, k45 (46, 47, 52, 53) sts of sleeve #1, k57 (59, 61, 65, 67) sts of the front; place the next 9 (10, 11, 10, 11) sts on a holder; k45 (46, 47, 52, 53) sts of sleeve #2, k57 (59, 61, 65, 67) sts of the back = a total of 204 (210, 216, 234, 240) sts.

Choose your color pattern and shape the yoke as shown on the chart (change to dpn when the sts no longer fit around the circular). After completing charted rows, 68 (70, 72, 78, 80) sts remain.

Neckband

With smaller size short circular or dpn, knit 1 rnd in desired color and, *at the same time*, decrease 14 (16, 16, 20, 20) sts evenly spaced around = a total of 54 (54, 56, 58, 60) sts remain. Work around in k1, p1 rib for 2¾-3¼ in / 7-8 cm and then bind off loosely. For other neckband options, see pages 14, 15, and 17.

Finishing

Weave in all ends neatly on WS. Seam the underarms with Kitchener stitch or three-needle bind-off (see page 8).

Fold down the doubled neckband to the WS and loosely sew the edge along neckline.

13

Sweaters with Ribbed Edgings

There are many options for ribbed edgings.

The most common ribbing is k1, p1.

Photos 1 and 2 show ribbing with a twisted knit.
K1, k1tbl (this stitch will be twisted because you bring the yarn through the back leg of the stitch instead of through the front).

Photo 3 shows k2, p2 rib (make sure you cast on a multiple of 4 sts for this ribbing).

Basic patterns—pages 11 and 13.
Chart—page 26.
You'll find even more alternatives for the edging on page 24.

Sweaters with Picot Edgings

Cast on the desired number of stitches with U.S. size 10 / 6 mm needles and join for working in the round. Work 5 rnds in stockinette. On the next rnd, *yo, k2tog (as when making a buttonhole); rep from * around. For an odd number of sts, beg with k1 before working * to *. On the next rnd, knit all the sts, including the yarnovers. Work 5 rnds in stockinette. Now continue with a single color or in a color pattern. To finish the picot edge, fold at the eyelet rnd and sew the cast-on edge to the inside of the sweater.

Basic patterns—pages 11 and 13.
Chart—page 26.
You'll find even more alternatives for the edging on page 24.

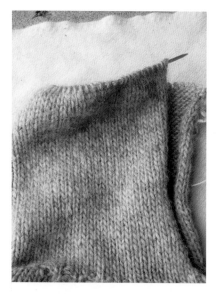

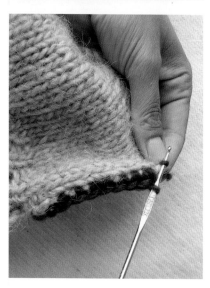

Hooded Sweaters

1 Follow your chosen pattern up to the neck. When you have the correct number of sts remaining on the needle (that is, after the final decreases), work 2-4 rnds in k1, p1 rib. Knit 1 rnd, increasing 10 sts evenly spaced around. Cut yarn. Attach yarn at center front and work back and forth in stockinette (knit on RS and purl on WS) until the hood is desired length.

2 Divide the stitches evenly over 2 needles. Hold the needles parallel to each other and k2tog (joining 1 st from each needle) and bind off *at the same time* (= three-needle bind-off, see page 8).

3 You can crochet an edging around the hood opening or you can pick up and knit sts and work a rib, garter stitch, or lace edging (see pages 14, 15, and 24 for these options).

4 Knitted-on edge
Begin at the lower edge on the right side of the hood. Pick up and knit 2 sts for every 3 rows all the way around to the left side of the hood.

Basic patterns—pages 11 and 13.
Chart—page 26.

Roll Collar Sweaters

1 Begin after the last decrease row of the chart (the 1st part of the pattern to the neck). Cut yarn. Attach yarn at center front and work in k1, p1 rib for ¾-1¼ in / 2-3 cm and then work back and forth in stockinette for about 2½ in / 6 cm (knit on RS and purl on WS). Cut yarn.

2 Fold the stockinette edge to the ribbed band with the wrong side facing out and sew it down.

3 Twist or braid a cord in chosen color and thread it through the casing around the neck.

Basic patterns—pages 11 and 13.
Chart—page 26.

CARDIGANS

Cardigans can be knit in the round following the instructions for the sweaters. The lower edge is worked back and forth on a circular needle and then the back and front are knit in the round up to the underarms. The sleeves can be knit in the round up to the underarm. After that, all the pieces are joined and the yoke is knit in the round over all the stitches. The front opening is then cut at the center front. The pieces can also be knit back and forth on a circular to avoid cutting at the center front. In that case, add an edge stitch at each side—the edge sts are knit on all rows.

The cast-on number depends on which button band you choose. Here are 3 options:

Cardigan with Button/Buttonhole Bands Sewn On

With smaller size circular, cast on 11 more stitches than specified for the body of a sweater pattern.
Work around in k1, p1 rib for ¾ in / 2 cm. Make a buttonhole, beginning on RS.

Right side of cardigan (for girls/women): Work 3 sts (= k1, p1, k1), yo, k2tog, continue in pattern as set.
Left side of cardigan (for boys/men): Work around until 4 sts remain on the round, yo, k2tog, complete round as set.

Next rnd: Continue in rib pattern until it measures approx 1½ (1½, 2, 2, 2½, 2½, 2½, 2¾, 2¾, 3¼) in / 4 (4, 5, 5, 6, 6, 6, 7, 7, 8) cm.

Place the first 6 sts on a holder. Change to larger size circular. Work around in stockinette, increasing evenly spaced around (as specified in the pattern) until 6 sts remain. Place the last 6 sts on a holder. Join piece to work in the round and, on the next rnd, increase 1 st at the beginning and 1 st at the end of the next rnd (2 center sts for later cutting). Purl these 2 center sts on all rounds. Work in the round up to the underarms.

Cardigan with Button/Buttonhole Bands Knitted On

Straight Model (without a ribbed band)

Cast on the number of stitches specified in the pattern, including the number of stitches increased following the ribbed band, + 1 st to balance the pattern. Do not join. Work in stockinette (or your choice of stitch pattern, see page 39). Work back and forth in pattern for 2 in / 5 cm. Purl 1 row on RS (for the foldline). Join piece to work in the round and continue in stockinette, *at the same time* adding 1 st at the beginning and 1 st at the end of the rnd (= 2 center or "steek" sts for later cutting). Purl these 2 center sts on all rounds. Work in the round up to the underarms.

Cardigan with Crocheted Button/Buttonhole Bands

Cast on the number of stitches specified in the pattern and work the ribbing back and forth. Now work around in stockinette, increasing evenly spaced around on the next round as indicated in the pattern, and adding 1 stitch to balance the pattern. *At the same time* as joining the piece to work in the round, add 1 st at the beginning and 1 st at the end of the first rnd (= 2 center or "steek" sts for later cutting). Purl these 2 center sts on all rounds. Work in the round up to the underarms.

Yoke

The cardigan pieces are assembled on the circular as for a sweater, but, begin at the left front.

Place all the pieces on the same circular as follows: With MC, p1, k21 (22, 23, 25, 27, 28, 29, 30, 32, 33) on the body, place the next 8 (8, 9, 8, 8, 9, 10, 11, 10, 11) sts on a holder, knit the 35 (38, 39, 41, 44, 45, 46, 47, 52, 53) sts of first sleeve, k43 (47, 49, 53, 55, 57, 59, 61, 65, 67) sts of body, place the next 8 (8, 9, 8, 8, 9, 10, 11, 10, 11) sts on a holder, k35 (38, 39, 41, 44, 45, 46, 47, 52, 53) sts of second sleeve, k21 (22, 23, 25, 27, 28, 29, 30, 32, 33) on the body, p1 = a total of 157 (169, 175, 187, 199, 205, 211, 217, 235, 241) sts. Work following the chart, decreasing as indicated on the chart. When stitches no longer fit around, change to a shorter circular. To reinforce center front before cutting open, machine-stitch 2 lines over the 2 center stitches and carefully cut open between the 2 stitches. Reinforce the raw edges with zigzag stitching on both sides.

Cardigan with Button/Buttonhole Bands Knitted On

1 Beginning at the lower edge, on the right side of the cardigan, pick up and knit 2 sts for every 3 rows along the edge up to the neckline.

2 Work 5 rows in stockinette for children's sizes or 7 rows for adult sizes, making the buttonholes at the same time. Make the buttonholes for girls and women on the right side of the sweater and on the left side for boys and men. Purl 1 row for the foldline. Work 8 (10) more rows in stockinette and then bind off. Make the other band the same way, omitting buttonholes.

3 Fold the band at the purl row and sew down on the WS, covering any raw edges. Sew on the buttons.

Basic patterns—pages 11 and 13.
Basic instructions for a cardigan—pages 18 and 19.
Chart—page 26.

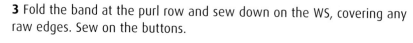

Cardigan with Button/Buttonhole Bands Sewn On

1 After you have reinforced and cut open the center front, place the 6 sts of the right buttonhole band on a needle. CO 3 sts for the edge. Work in knit and purl as for the beginning of the band and then work the 3 sts that you just added in stockinette (knit on the RS and purl on the WS). Continue until the band, when slightly stretched, reaches the neckline. BO the 3 stockinette sts and place the remaining 6 sts on a holder. Work the left band the same way.

Note: Don't forget to make the buttonholes on the correct side of the cardigan: on the left side for boys/men and on the right for girls/women.

2 With RS facing, sew on the button/buttonhole bands. Make sure that the 3-stitch panel lies on the WS.

3 Place the 6 sts of the button band on a circular. Work around the neck in ribbing (decrease x the number of stitches specified in the pattern), place the 6 sts of left band on the circular. Work back and forth in ribbing as set until neckband is desired length.

4 Sew the 3-st panel of each buttonhole/button band on WS to cover raw edges.

Basic patterns—pages 11 and 13.
Basic instructions for a cardigan—pages 18 and 19.
Chart—page 26.

Cardigan with Pockets and Crocheted Button/Buttonhole Bands

1 Beginning at the lower edge, on the right side of the cardigan, work single crochet (sc) into every other row up to the collar.

2 Turn and work sc in every stitch back to the lower edge.

3 Crochet the buttonholes (**Note:** make buttonholes on the left side for boys/men and on the right for girls/women). Mark the spacing of the buttonholes (the number of buttonholes depends on the size of the garment—for example, 5 for children's sizes and 7 for adults). Buttonhole: Skip 1 st and ch 2.

4 On the sweater shown here, the last row is worked with a contrast color. Beginning at the lower edge, on the right side, work in sc up to the collar and then down to the lower edge of the left front.

5 Sew on buttons.

Basic patterns—pages 11 and 13.
Basic instructions for a cardigan—pages 18 and 19.
Chart—page 26.

Pockets

1 Work the body of the sweater up to the pocket opening. Cast on 32 (40) sts on a U.S. 10 / 6 mm double-pointed needle (dpn); divide sts evenly over 4 dpn. Join and work around in stockinette for approx 3½ (4¾) in / 9 (12) cm. Divide the sts onto 2 dpn = 16 (20) sts on each needle. Turn the pocket wrong side out. After you've determined the placement of the pocket, place the pocket behind the body.

2 Knit 3 together (= 1 st from the body, 1 st from the front of the pocket, and 1 st from the back of the pocket).

3 Knit 2 together = the 2 first sts on the needles (1 st from the body and 1 st from the front of the pocket). Continue to knit and bind off the sts of the body with those on the front of the pocket.

4 When 16 (20) sts have been bound off, the piece should look like the example shown in the photo to the right. Move the last st from the pocket to the circular. Work across to the next pocket. Repeat from figure 1.

Various Edgings

Straight Models
Cast on the number of stitches specified in the pattern, plus the number of stitches that would be added after a ribbed edging.

If you want the edge to be a bit tighter than the body, work the edge with smaller needles—for example, U.S. 7 / 4.5 mm.

Seed Stitch
Row 1: *K1, p1*.
Row 2: Work purl over knit and knit over purl.
Repeat Rows 1-2.

Stockinette Edging
In the round on a circular needle: Knit all rows.

Back and forth on 2 needles: Knit on the RS and purl on the WS.

Note: this edge rolls up somewhat.

Garter Stitch Edging
Knit all rows back and forth.

Yarn Amounts for Models Knitted in the Round

	5 yrs	7 yrs	9 yrs	10 yrs	12 yrs	XS	S	M	L	XL
Model 1										
Main Color	3	4	4	5	5	6	7	7	8	8
A	1	1	1	1	1	1	1	1	1	1
B	1	1	1	1	1	1	1	1	1	1
C	1	1	1	1	1	1	1	1	1	1
D	1	1	1	1	1	1	1	1	1	1
Model 2										
Main Color	3	4	4	5	5	6	7	7	8	8
A	1	1	1	1	1	1	1	1	1	1
B	1	1	1	1	1	1	1	1	1	1
C	1	1	1	1	1	1	1	1	1	1
Model 3, 4 colors										
Main Color										
A		2		2		2		2		2
B		3		3		4		4		4
C		2		2		3		3		3
D		1		1		2		2		3
Model 3, 2 colors										
A		5		7		9		10		10
B		1		1		1		2		2
Model 4										
Main Color						5	6	6	7	7
A						2	3	3	3	3
B						1	1	1	1	1
Model 5, 4 colors										
Main Color	3	4	4	5	5	5	5	5	6	6
A	1	1	1	1	2	2	3	3	4	4
B	1	1	1	1	1	1	1	1	2	2
C	1	1	1	1	1	1	1	1	1	1
Model 5, 3 colors										
A	3	4	4	5	5	5	5	5	6	6
B	1	1	1	1	2	2	3	3	4	4
C	1	1	1	1	1	1	1	1	1	2
Model 6										
Main Color	3	4	5	5	6	7	7	7	8	8
A	1	1	1	1	1	2	2	2	2	2
B	1	1	1	1	1	1	1	1	2	2
Model 7, 2 colors										
Main Color	3	4	4	5	6	7	7	7	8	8
A	1	1	1	1	1	1	2	2	2	2
Model 7, 5 colors										
Main Color	3	3	3	4	5	6	6	6	7	7
A	1	1	1	1	1	1	2	2	2	2
B	1	1	1	1	1	1	1	1	1	1
C	1	1	1	1	1	1	1	1	1	1
D	1	1	1	1	1	1	1	1	1	1

Model 1

Child

5 yrs: skip Row 35
52 (56, 58, 62, 66) sts

5 (7, 9, 10) yrs: skip Row 32

[O] = Main Color
78 (84, 87, 93, 99) sts
5 (7, 9) yrs: skip Row 29

5 yrs: skip Row 26
[●] = Main Color
5 (7, 9, 10) yrs: skip Row 24

5 (7) yrs: skip Row 20

5 (7, 9) yrs: skip Row 19
104 (112, 116, 124, 132) sts

5 (7) yrs: skip Row 14

130 (140, 145, 155, 165) sts

[●] = Main Color
5 (7, 9, 10, 12) yrs: begin here
156 (168, 174, 186, 198) sts
(Cardigan + 1 st on all sizes)

[◰] K2tog

[▩] No stitch

[ ] = Main Color
[●] = A
[O] = B
[■] = C
[X] = D

Adult

68 (70, 72, 78, 80) sts
XS (S, M, L,): skip Row 41

102 (105, 108, 117, 120) sts

XS (S): skip Row 32

XS: skip Row 27
136 (140, 144, 156, 160) sts

XS (S, M, L): skip Row 22

170 (175, 180, 195, 200) sts

XS (S, M): skip Row 15

XS (S, M): skip Row 8

XS (S, M, L): skip Row 1
204 (210, 216, 234, 240) sts
(Cardigan: + 1 st on all sizes)

repeat
center front

XL
5 (9) yrs   M   12 yrs
S   L XS

[▪] = purl on all rnds (1-43)
begin cardigan

Row numbers (Child left / Adult right):
35/43, 34/42, 33/41, 32/40, 31/39, 30/38, 29/37, 28/36, 27/35, 26/34, 25/33, 24/32, 23/31, 22/30, 21/29, 20/28, 19/27, 18/26, 17/25, 16/24, 15/23, 14/22, 13/21, 12/20, 11/19, 10/18, 9/17, 8/16, 7/15, 6/14, 5/13, 4/12, 3/11, 2/10, 1/9, 8, 7, 6, 5, 4, 3, 2, 1

26

SWEATER OPTIONS

The characteristic Lopi sweater, with its two-color patterns on a circularly-knit yoke, has achieved national status relatively quickly—it was only in the 1950s that the first Lopi sweaters were knitted in Iceland. Originally we only used natural sheep's wool colors for the motifs. Now you'll find a large range of colors and many pattern variations. However, even the oldest models are still in style. The models shown in the next few pages feature a combination of old and new pattern bands.

Model 2

Child

Adult

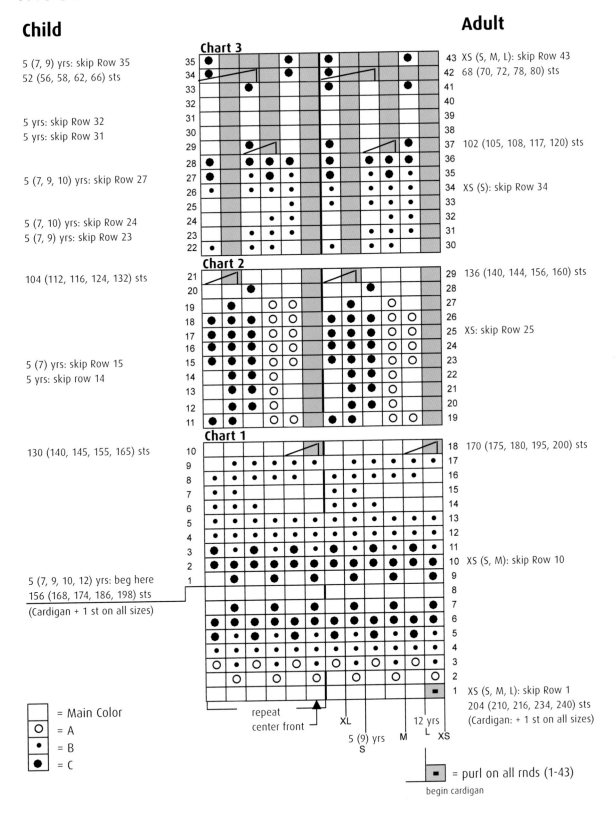

Chart 3

5 (7, 9) yrs: skip Row 35
52 (56, 58, 62, 66) sts

43 — XS (S, M, L): skip Row 43
42 — 68 (70, 72, 78, 80) sts

5 yrs: skip Row 32
5 yrs: skip Row 31

37 — 102 (105, 108, 117, 120) sts

5 (7, 9, 10) yrs: skip Row 27

34 — XS (S): skip Row 34

5 (7, 10) yrs: skip Row 24
5 (7, 9) yrs: skip Row 23

Chart 2

104 (112, 116, 124, 132) sts

29 — 136 (140, 144, 156, 160) sts

25 — XS: skip Row 25

5 (7) yrs: skip Row 15
5 yrs: skip row 14

Chart 1

130 (140, 145, 155, 165) sts

18 — 170 (175, 180, 195, 200) sts

10 — XS (S, M): skip Row 10

5 (7, 9, 10, 12) yrs: beg here
156 (168, 174, 186, 198) sts
(Cardigan + 1 st on all sizes)

1 — XS (S, M, L): skip Row 1
204 (210, 216, 234, 240) sts
(Cardigan: + 1 st on all sizes)

repeat
center front

XL

5 (9) yrs
S

M
L

12 yrs
XS

☐ = Main Color
Ⓞ = A
• = B
● = C

▪ = purl on all rnds (1-43)
begin cardigan

29

Model 2

☐ = Main Color
⊙ = A
⊙ = B
⬤ = C

Child

104 (112, 116, 124, 132) sts

5 yrs: skip Row 17

5 (7) yrs: skip Row 14

Chart 4

Adult

136 (140, 144, 156, 160) sts

XS: skip Row 25

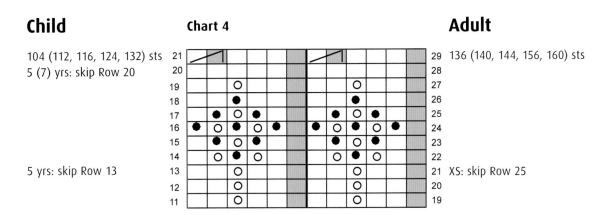

	= Main Color
O	= A
•	= B
●	= C

Child

Chart 4

Adult

104 (112, 116, 124, 132) sts

5 (7) yrs: skip Row 20

5 yrs: skip Row 13

136 (140, 144, 156, 160) sts

XS: skip Row 25

Model 3

Sizes: 5-7 yrs (9-10, 12) years; XS (S/M, L/LX)

Body

With U.S. 10 / 6 mm circular, CO 54 (60, 66, 72, 78) sts. Work back and forth in stockinette for 5 rows (knit on RS and purl on WS), but knit the first and last st on each row. Now work Chart 1 A. Cut yarn and work another piece the same way. Put the pieces on a circular = 108 (120, 132, 144, 156) sts. Work Chart 1 B, Chart 2 and Chart 3. Do not knit the last 4 (5, 5, 6, 6) sts of the last rnd. Do *not* cut yarn. Set piece aside and make sleeves.

Sleeves

With U.S. 10 / 6 mm dpn, CO 36 (36, 36, 42, 42) sts. Join and work 5 rnds stockinette. Work Chart 1 A, Chart 1 B, Chart 2 and Chart 3. Increase 2 sts at the center of underarm, 1 time on Rnd 1 of Chart 2 and then on every 5th rnd for sizes 5-10 years, on every 6th rnd for sizes 12 years-XL, 4 (6, 8, 7, 10) times = 46 (50, 54, 58, 64) sts total. Place the last 4 (4, 5, 6, 6) sts and the first 4 (4, 5, 5, 5) sts of the round on a holder. Make the second sleeve the same way.

Yoke

Join the sleeves and body as follows: Place the last 4 (5, 5, 6, 6) sts and the first 4 (4, 5, 5, 5) sts of the round from the body onto a holder. With color A and circular U.S. 10 / 6 mm, k38 (41, 44, 47, 53) sts of sleeve #1, k46 (51, 56, 61, 67) sts of the front, place the next 8 (9, 10, 10, 11, 11) from the body on a holder, k38 (41, 44, 47, 53) sts of sleeve #2, k46 (51, 56, 61, 67) sts of the back = a total of 168 (184, 200, 216, 240) sts. Work Charts 4 A and 4 B, decreasing as indicated on the charts. Change to dpn when stitches no longer fit around circular. After completing charted rows, 66 (72, 81, 87, 96) sts remain.

Hood

Begin at center front at the neck opening. Work back and forth, decreasing 7 (1, 0, 6, 15) sts on the first row. Work Chart 4 A, beginning on Row 7 and working Rows 7-17 a total of 5 times for sizes 5-10 yrs, and a total of 6 times for sizes 12 years-XL. Work Chart 4 A, Rows 1-4. Divide the sts over 2 needles. Hold the needles parallel and, using a third needle, work three-needle bind-off (see page 8).

Cables

See Symbol Key for Chart 2—Cables
Slash from right to left: Place the first 2 sts on a cable needle and hold in front of work, knit the next 2 sts and then knit the 2 sts on cable needle.
Slash from left to right: Place the first 2 sts on a cable needle and hold behind work, knit the next 2 sts and then knit the 2 sts on cable needle.

Model 3

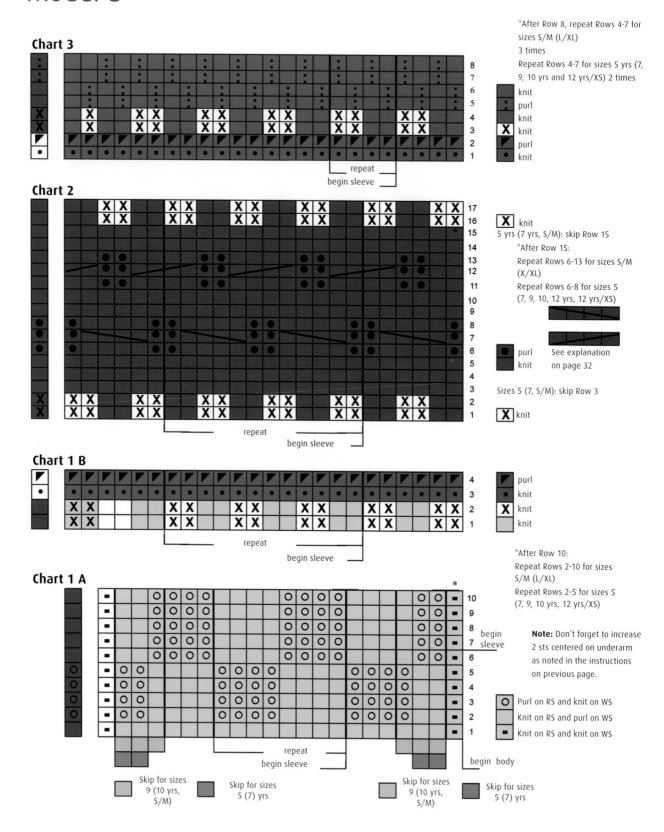

Chart 3

8
7
6
5
4
3
2
1

repeat
begin sleeve

*After Row 8, repeat Rows 4-7 for sizes S/M (L/XL)
3 times
Repeat Rows 4-7 for sizes 5 yrs (7, 9, 10 yrs and 12 yrs/XS) 2 times

☐ knit
☐ purl
☐ knit
X knit
◤ purl
• knit

Chart 2

17
16
15
14
13
12
11
10
9
8
7
6
5
4
3
2
1

repeat
begin sleeve

X knit
5 yrs (7 yrs, S/M): skip Row 15
*After Row 15:
Repeat Rows 6-13 for sizes S/M (X/XL)
Repeat Rows 6-8 for sizes 5 (7, 9, 10, 12 yrs, 12 yrs/XS)

• purl   See explanation
☐ knit   on page 32

Sizes 5 (7, S/M): skip Row 3

X knit

Chart 1 B

4
3
2
1

repeat
begin sleeve

◤ purl
• knit
X knit
☐ knit

*After Row 10:
Repeat Rows 2-10 for sizes S/M (L/XL)
Repeat Rows 2-5 for sizes 5 (7, 9, 10 yrs, 12 yrs/XS)

Note: Don't forget to increase 2 sts centered on underarm as noted in the instructions on previous page.

Chart 1 A

10
9
8   begin
7   sleeve
6
5
4
3
2
1

repeat
begin sleeve   begin body

O Purl on RS and knit on WS
☐ Knit on RS and purl on WS
■ Knit on RS and knit on WS

Skip for sizes   Skip for sizes   Skip for sizes   Skip for sizes
9 (10 yrs,   5 (7) yrs   9 (10 yrs,   5 (7) yrs
S/M)   S/M)

34

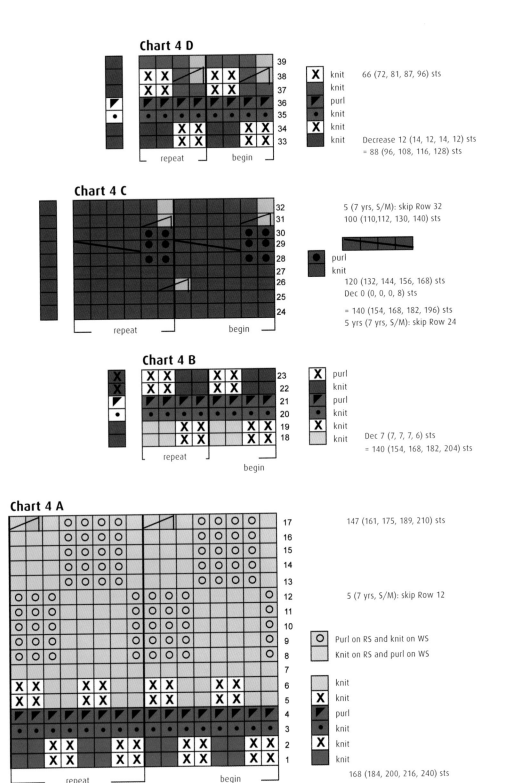

Chart 4 D

knit — 66 (72, 81, 87, 96) sts
knit
purl
knit
knit
knit — Decrease 12 (14, 12, 14, 12) sts = 88 (96, 108, 116, 128) sts

repeat   begin

Chart 4 C

5 (7 yrs, S/M): skip Row 32
100 (110,112, 130, 140) sts

purl
knit

120 (132, 144, 156, 168) sts
Dec 0 (0, 0, 0, 8) sts

= 140 (154, 168, 182, 196) sts
5 yrs (7 yrs, S/M): skip Row 24

repeat   begin

Chart 4 B

purl
knit
purl
knit
knit
knit — Dec 7 (7, 7, 7, 6) sts = 140 (154, 168, 182, 204) sts

repeat   begin

Chart 4 A

147 (161, 175, 189, 210) sts

5 (7 yrs, S/M): skip Row 12

Purl on RS and knit on WS
Knit on RS and purl on WS

knit
knit
purl
knit
knit
knit

168 (184, 200, 216, 240) sts

repeat   begin

35

Model 4

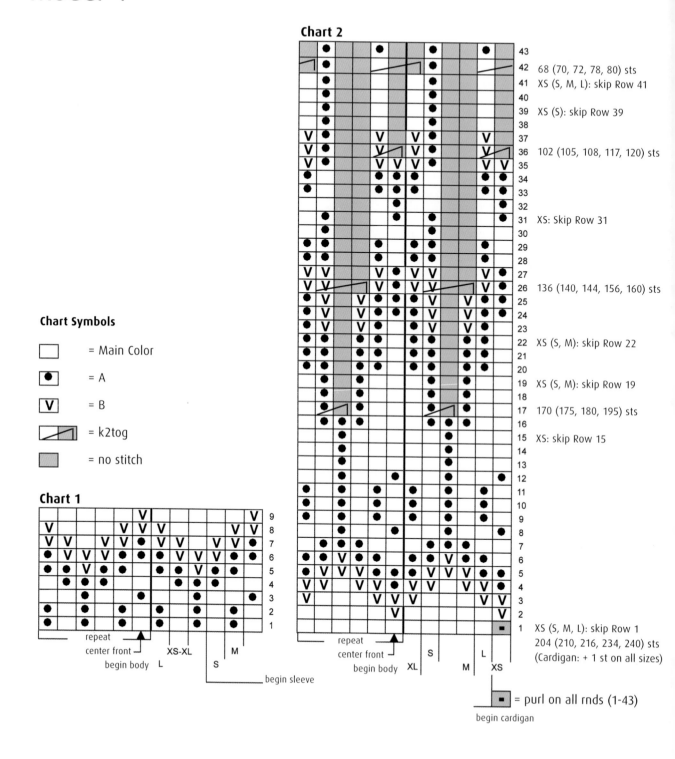

Chart 2

68 (70, 72, 78, 80) sts
XS (S, M, L): skip Row 41

XS (S): skip Row 39

102 (105, 108, 117, 120) sts

XS: Skip Row 31

136 (140, 144, 156, 160) sts

XS (S, M): skip Row 22

XS (S, M): skip Row 19

170 (175, 180, 195) sts

XS: skip Row 15

Chart Symbols

☐	= Main Color
●	= A
V	= B
◰	= k2tog
▨	= no stitch

Chart 1

repeat
center front
begin body L   S
XS-XL   M
begin sleeve

repeat
center front
begin body XL   S   L   XS
M

XS (S, M, L): skip Row 1
204 (210, 216, 234, 240) sts
(Cardigan: + 1 st on all sizes)

■ = purl on all rnds (1-43)

begin cardigan

Model 5

Child

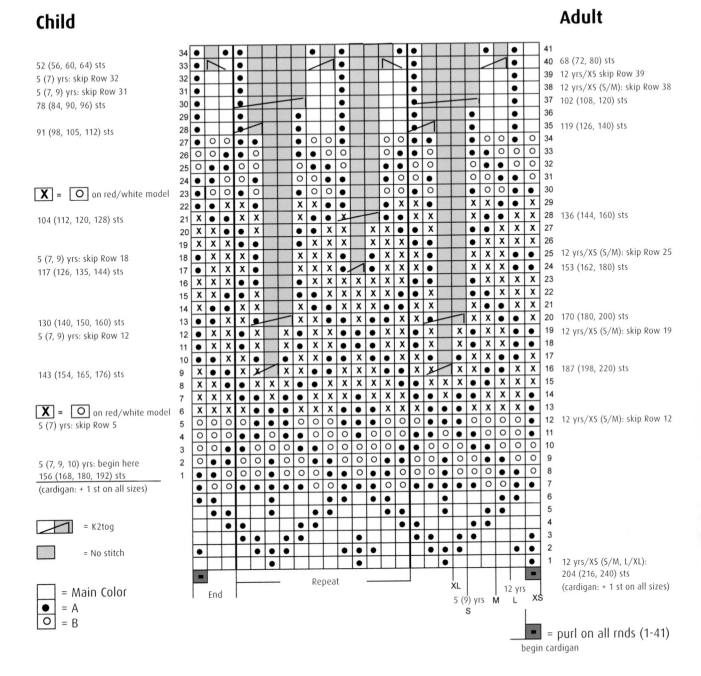

52 (56, 60, 64) sts
5 (7) yrs: skip Row 32
5 (7, 9) yrs: skip Row 31
78 (84, 90, 96) sts

91 (98, 105, 112) sts

$\boxed{X}$ = $\boxed{O}$ on red/white model

104 (112, 120, 128) sts

5 (7, 9) yrs: skip Row 18
117 (126, 135, 144) sts

130 (140, 150, 160) sts
5 (7, 9) yrs: skip Row 12

143 (154, 165, 176) sts

$\boxed{X}$ = $\boxed{O}$ on red/white model
5 (7) yrs: skip Row 5

5 (7, 9, 10) yrs: begin here
156 (168, 180, 192) sts
(cardigan: + 1 st on all sizes)

= K2tog

= No stitch

= Main Color
● = A
○ = B

Adult

68 (72, 80) sts
12 yrs/XS skip Row 39
12 yrs/XS (S/M): skip Row 38
102 (108, 120) sts

119 (126, 140) sts

136 (144, 160) sts

12 yrs/XS (S/M): skip Row 25
153 (162, 180) sts

170 (180, 200) sts
12 yrs/XS (S/M): skip Row 19

187 (198, 220) sts

12 yrs/XS (S/M): skip Row 12

End · Repeat

XL · 12 yrs
5 (9) yrs · M · L · XS
S

12 yrs/XS (S/M, L/XL):
204 (216, 240) sts
(cardigan: + 1 st on all sizes)

■ = purl on all rnds (1-41)
begin cardigan

Note:
Child sizes: 5 (7, 9, 10) years
Sizes 9 (9-10) years: CO 6 sts more than specified in the basic pattern
Sizes 10 (10-12) years: CO 6 fewer sts than specified in the basic pattern
After completing all charted rows, 52 (56, 60, 64) sts remain

Model 6

Child

5 (7, 9) yrs: skip Row 35
52 (56, 58, 62, 66) sts

5 yrs: skip Row 32
5 yrs: Skip Row 31
78 (84, 87, 93, 99) sts

5 (7, 9, 10) yrs: skip Row 27

5 (7, 9, 10) yrs: skip Row 24
5 (7, 9) yrs: skip Row 23

5 (7, 9) yrs: skip Row 21

104 (112, 116, 124, 132) sts

5 (7, 9) yrs: skip Row 14

130 (140, 145, 155, 165) sts

5 (7, 9, 10, 12) yrs: begin here
156 (168, 174, 186, 198) sts
(Cardigan + 1 st on all sizes)

Adult

43 XS: skip Row 43
42 68 (70, 72, 78, 80) sts
41 XS (S, M): skip Row 41
40 XS (S, M, L): skip Row 40

38 102 (105,108, 117, 120) sts

36 XS (S, M): skip Row 36

30 XS (S): skip Row 30

27 136 (140, 156, 160) sts

22 XS (S, M, L): skip Row 22

18 170 (175, 180, 195, 200) sts

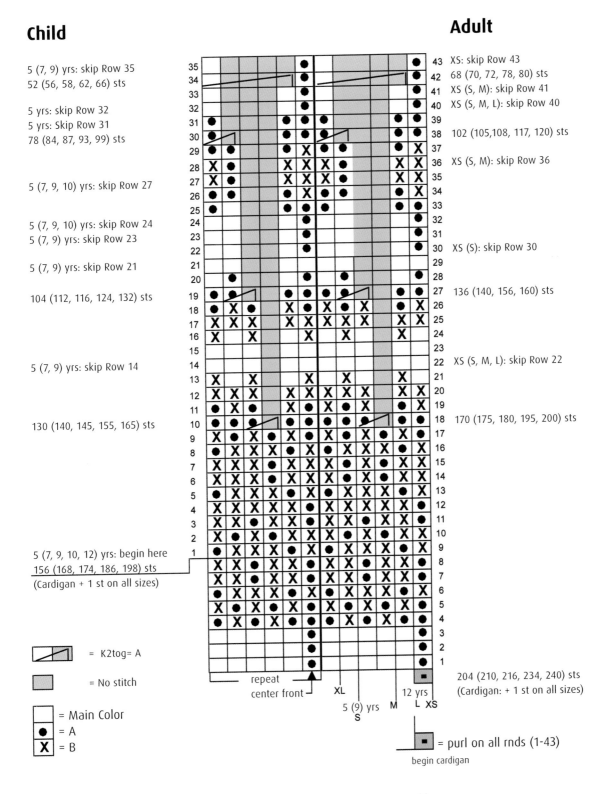

= K2tog= A

= No stitch

= Main Color

● = A

X = B

repeat
center front

XL

5 (9) yrs   M
S

12 yrs
L XS

204 (210, 216, 234, 240) sts
(Cardigan: + 1 st on all sizes)

= purl on all rnds (1-43)

begin cardigan

41

Model 7

Child

5 (7, 9, 10) yrs: skip Row 35
52 (56, 58, 62, 66) sts

78 (84, 87, 93, 99) sts

5 (7, 9) yrs: skip Row 30

5 (7, 9, 10) yrs: skip Row 27

5 (7, 10) yrs: skip Row 24
104 (112, 116, 124, 132) sts

5 (7, 9) yrs: skip Row 21

5 (7, 9) yrs: skip Row 14
5 (7): skip Row 13

130 (140, 145, 155, 165) sts

5 (7, 9, 10, 12) yrs: begin here
156 (168, 174, 186, 198) sts
(Cardigan + 1 st on all sizes)

Adult

43 XS (S, M, L): skip Row 43
42 68 (70, 72, 78, 80) sts

40 102 (105, 108, 117, 120) sts

35 XS (S): skip Row 35

31 136 (140, 144, 156, 160) sts

29 XS: skip Row 29

22 XS (S, M, L): skip Row 22

19 170 (175, 180, 195, 200) sts

8 XS (S, M): skip Row 8

1 XS (S, M, L): Skip Row 1
204 (210, 216, 234, 240) sts
(cardigan: + 1 st on all sizes)

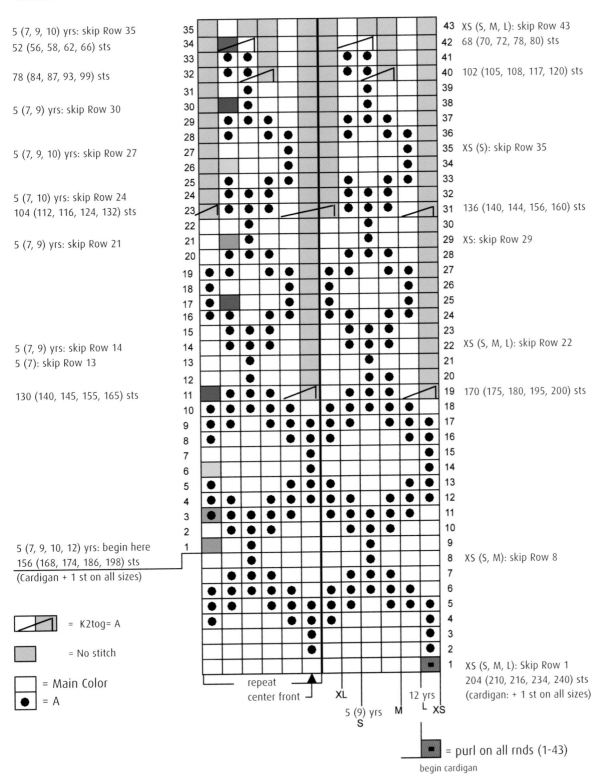

= K2tog= A

= No stitch

= Main Color

• = A

repeat
center front

XL

5 (9) yrs   M
S

12 yrs
L   XS

= purl on all rnds (1-43)

begin cardigan

ACCESSORIES

This section features basic patterns for hats, mittens, and bags. With only a few small changes, you can make your own completely personal variations on these garments. Decorate them with buttons, patches, tassels, etc.

Your outfit will be especially exciting if you match your sweater or cardigan with a hat and bag.

Hat—Basic Pattern

Sizes: 5-7 yrs (8-12 yrs, adult)
Gauge: 13 sts and 18 rnds on needles U.S. 10 / 6 mm = 4 x 4 in / 10 x 10 cm
Yarn: CYCA #5, 100 g = 109 yd / 100 m
Yarn amount: 100 g

The hat is knit in the round on U.S. 10 / 6 mm needles.
CO 60 (63, 66) sts with the color you like. Join, being careful not to twist cast-on row.
Work around in stockinette (knit all rounds) for 8 (8¼, 8¾) in / 20 (21, 22) cm.
Top shaping:
1st dec round: *K1, k2tog*; rep from * to * around = 40 (42, 44) sts remain.
Knit 3 rounds without decreasing.
2nd dec round: *K2tog*; rep from * to * around = 20 (21, 22) sts remain.
Knit 2 rounds without decreasing.
3rd dec round: *K2tog*; rep from * to * around until 5 (6, 6) sts remain.
Cut yarn and draw end through remaining 5 (6, 6) sts; pull tight. Weave in all ends neatly on WS.

Beanie

The beanie is worked as for the basic hat but has an edge with a facing rather than a rolled edge.

Begin as for basic hat and work 5 (5, 6) rnds in stockinette. Purl 1 round (foldline) and then continue in stockinette, following the pattern for the basic hat. Finish by folding around the edge at the purl round and sewing the facing down loosely on WS. Weave in all ends neatly on WS.

Make a pompom and attach it securely where you like.

Stocking Cap

Sizes: 5-12 yrs (adult)
Gauge: 13 sts and 18 rnds on needles U.S. 10 / 6 mm = 4 x 4 in / 10 x 10 cm
Yarn: CYCA #5, 100 g = 109 yd / 100 m
Yarn amount: MC: 200 g; CC: 100 g

The cap is knit in the round on U.S. 10 / 6 mm needles.
CO 60 (66) sts; join, being careful not to twist cast-on row.
Work around in stockinette (knit all rounds) for approx 2 (2¾) in / 5 (7) cm and then turn work inside out.

Continue in stockinette until piece measures 6 (6¼) in / 15 (16) cm long from foldline.

1st dec round: *K4, k2tog*; rep from * to * around = 50 (55) sts remain.
Work in stockinette for approx 4 (5½) in / 10 (14) cm without decreasing.
2nd dec round: *K3, k2tog*; rep from * to * around = 40 (44) sts remain.
Work in stockinette for approx 4 (5½) in / 10 (14) cm without decreasing.
3rd dec round: *K2, k2tog*; rep from * to * around = 30 (33) sts remain.
Work in stockinette for approx 4 (5½) in / 10 (14) cm without decreasing.
4th dec round: *K1, k2tog*; rep from * to * around = 20 (22) sts remain.
Work in stockinette for approx 3¼ (4¾) in / 8 (12) cm without decreasing.
5th dec round: *K2tog*; rep from * to * around = 10 (11) sts remain.
Knit 2 rounds in stockinette and then repeat Rnd 5 = 5 (6) sts remain.
Cut yarn and pull end through remaining 5 (6) sts; pull tight. Turn cap under at the foldline and sew the facing down with loose sts on WS. Weave in all ends neatly on WS.

If you want a longer cap, knit more rounds between each decrease round.

45

Beret/Tam

Sizes:	child (adult)
Gauge:	13 sts and 18 rnds on needles U.S. 10 / 6 mm = 4 x 4 in / 10 x 10 cm
Yarn:	CYCA #5, 100 g = 109 yd / 100 m
Yarn amount:	100 g

The beret is knit in the round on U.S. 10 / 6 mm needles.

CO 52 (56) sts with the color you prefer; join, being careful not to twist cast-on row. Work 2 rnds in k1, p1 rib.

Rnd 3: K1 (0), *M1, k1*; rep from * to * around = 103 (112) sts.
Rnd 4: Knit around (no increases).
Rnd 5: *M1, k6*; rep from * to * around and end k1 (4) = 120 (130) sts.

Continue in stockinette until piece is 5¼ (6) in / 13 (15) cm long.

1st dec round: *K10 (11), k2tog*; rep from * to * around.
2nd dec round: *K9 (10), k2tog*; rep from * to * around = 110 (120) sts remain.
3rd dec round: *K8 (9), k2tog*; rep from * to * around = 100 (110) sts remain.
Continue decreasing on every round, with 1 less st between decreases on each rnd, until 10 sts remain.

Next rnd: *K2tog*; rep from * to * around = 5 sts remain.
Knit 3 more rounds without decreasing.
Cut yarn and draw end through remaining 5 sts; pull tight. Weave in all ends neatly on WS.

Earflap Hat

Sizes:	child (adult)
Gauge:	13 sts and 18 rnds on needles U.S. 10 / 6 mm = 4 x 4 in / 10 x 10 cm
Yarn:	CYCA #5, 100 g = 109 yd / 100 m
Yarn amount:	100 g

The earflaps are worked back and forth and the rest of the hat is knit in the round.

Earflaps (make two alike)
CO 3 (5) sts in chosen color. Work back and forth in stockinette, increasing at each side as shown on the chart = 15 (17) sts.

Hat
With RS facing and your choice of color, K15 (17) over 1st earflap, CO 24 (25) sts, k15 (17) over 2nd earflap, CO 12 (13) sts = 66 (72) sts total. Work around in stockinette until hat measures approx 5¼ (6) in / 13 (15) cm.

Top Shaping/Finishing
1st dec round: *K1, k2tog*; rep from * to * around = 44 (48) sts remain.
Knit 3 rounds without decreasing.
2nd dec round: *K2tog*; rep from * to * around = 22 (24) sts remain.
Knit 2 rounds without decreasing.
2nd dec round: *K2tog*; rep from * to * around until 6 sts remain. Cut yarn and draw end through remaining 6 sts; pull tight. Weave in all ends neatly on WS.

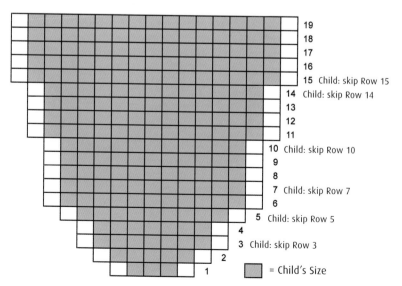

19
18
17
16
15 Child: skip Row 15
14 Child: skip Row 14
13
12
11
10 Child: skip Row 10
9
8
7 Child: skip Row 7
6
5 Child: skip Row 5
4
3 Child: skip Row 3
2
1

⬛ = Child's Size

Afghan-Style Cap

Sizes: child (adult)
Gauge: 13 sts and 18 rnds
           on needles U.S. 10 /
           6 mm = 4 x 4 in /
           10 x 10 cm
Yarn: CYCA #5, 100 g =
           109 yd / 100 m
Yarn amount: 100 g

The cap is worked in the round on U.S. 10 / 6 mm needles. Change to dpn when the sts no longer fit around circular.

With your choice of color, CO 54 (60) sts; join, being careful not to twist cast-on row. Work 2 rnds in k1, p1 rib and then work in stockinette for 2½ (3½) in / 6 (9) cm. Turn work inside out. Continue in stockinette until piece measures 5¼ (6¼) in / 13 (16) cm.

1st inc round: *K1, M1, k7 (8), M1, k1*; rep from * to * around = 66 (72) sts.

Knit 3 rnds without increasing.
2nd inc round: *K2, M1, k7 (8), M1, k2*; rep from * to * around = 78 (84) sts.
Knit 3 rnds without increasing.
3rd inc round: *K3, M1, k7 (8), M1, k3*; rep from * to * around = 90 (96) sts.
Continue in stockinette until piece measures 8 (10¼) in / 20 (26) cm. Knit 1 rnd with a contrast color, purl 1 rnd, knit 1 rnd.

Top Shaping:
1st dec rnd: *K1, k2tog, k9 (10), k2tog, k1*; rep from * to * around = 78 (84) sts remain.
Knit 3 rnds without decreasing.
2nd dec rnd: *K1, k2tog, k7 (8), k2tog, k1*; rep from * to * around = 66 (72) sts remain.
Knit 3 rnds without decreasing.
3rd dec rnd: *K1, k2tog, k5 (6), k2tog, k1*; rep from * to * around = 54 (60) sts remain.
Knit 3 rnds without decreasing.
4th dec rnd: *K1, k2tog, k3 (4), k2tog, k1*; rep from * to * around = 42 (48) sts remain.
Knit 3 rnds without decreasing.
5th dec rnd: *K1, k2tog, k1 (2), k2tog, k1*; rep from * to * around = 30 (36) sts remain.
Knit 3 rnds without decreasing.
6th dec rnd: *K2tog*; rep from * to * around = 15 (18) sts remain.
7th dec rnd: *K2tog* around until approx 6 sts remain.
Cut yarn and draw end through remaining sts; pull tight. Weave in all ends neatly on WS.

Socks—Basic Pattern

Sizes: 4-5 yrs (6-8 yrs, 10-12 yrs, women, men)
Gauge: 13 sts and 18 rnds on needles U.S. 10 / 6 mm = 4 x 4 in /
                10 x 10 cm
Yarn: CYCA #5, 100 g = 109 yd / 100 m
Yarn amount: 100 g

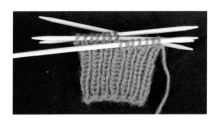

The socks shown in the photos are knitted with a heavy wool yarn. For more durable socks, you might want to choose a yarn that is a blend of wool and nylon which will be stronger.

With dpn U.S. 10 / 6 mm, CO 28 (32, 36, 42, 46) sts and divide onto 4 dpn; join, being careful not to twist cast-on row.

Work in k1, p1 rib for 4¾ (5½, 6¼, 8, 9½) in / 12 (14, 16, 20, 24) cm.

Work 1 rnd in stockinette, decreasing with k2tog 4 (4, 4, 6, 6) times evenly spaced around = 24 (28, 32, 36, 40) sts. Continue in stockinette for 1¼ (1½, 2, 2½, 2¾) in / 3 (4, 5, 6, 7) cm.

Heel

Move the sts from needle 1 onto ndl 4 = 12 (14, 16, 18, 20) sts for the heel. Work the heel back and forth in stockinette. Always begin every row with slip 1 purlwise with yarn held behind. Work 10 (12, 14, 16, 18) rows so that there will 5 (6, 7, 8, 9) edge sts. End the stockinette so that you can begin decreasing for the heel on the WS.

Row 1: P7 (8, 10, 11, 13), p2tog; turn.
Row 2: Sl 1 purlwise wyb, k2 (2, 4, 4, 6), ssk; turn.
Row 3: Sl 1 purlwise wyb, p2 (2, 4, 4, 6), p2tog; turn.
Row 4: Sl 1 purlwise wyb, k2 (2, 4, 4, 6), ssk; turn.
Continue the same way until you've worked all the sts on both sides.

Divide the heel sts onto 2 dpn. Pick up and knit 5 (6, 7, 8, 9) sts along each side of the heel flap and return to knitting in the round. Dec 1 st on each side of the heel at instep on every other rnd until 6 (7, 8, 9, 10) sts remain on each of the 4 dpn = 24 (28, 32, 36, 40) sts total. Continue around in stockinette until foot measures approx 3½ (4¼, 4¾, 5¼, 5½) in / 9 (11, 12, 13, 14) cm or to desired length.

Toe

Dpn 1 and 3: Knit until 3 sts remain on needle and k2tog, k1.
Dpn 2 and 4: K1, ssk, knit to end of needle.
Decrease for the toe on every other rnd 2 (2, 3, 3, 4) times and then on every rnd until 8 sts remain. Cut yarn and draw end through remaining 6 sts; pull tight. Weave in all ends neatly on WS.

Mittens—Basic Pattern

Sizes: 5-6 yrs (7-9 yrs, 10-12 yrs, women, men)
Gauge: 13 sts and 18 rnds on needles U.S. 10 / 6 mm = 4 x 4 in / 10 x 10 cm
Yarn: CYCA #5, 100 g = 109 yd / 100 m
Yarn amount: 100 g

1 Right Mitten

With smaller size needles, CO 20 (20, 22, 24, 28) sts and divide over 4 dpn; join, being careful not to twist cast-on row. Work in k1, p1 rib for approx 2 (2, 2½, 2¾, 2¾) in / 5 (5, 6, 7, 7) cm.
Change to larger dpn and stockinette. On the first rnd, inc 0 (2, 2, 4, 4) sts evenly spaced around = 20 (22, 24, 28, 32) sts. Place a marker between the first and last st of the rnd and between the 10th/11th (11th/12th, 12th/13th, 14th/15th, 16th/17th) sts and move markers up every rnd. Knit 9 (10, 11, 12, 12) rnds.

2 Thumbhole

Knit the first 4 (4, 5, 5, 6) sts of the rnd with smooth contrast color yarn. Move these sts back to the left needle and knit again with pattern yarn. Continue knitting in the round for approx 5¼ (5½, 6, 7, 8) in / 13 (14, 15, 18, 20) cm from the end of the ribbing.

3-4 Shaping the Top of the Mitten

Rnd 1: *Slip the first st of the round, knit the next st and pass slipped st over (or work ssk). Knit across until 2 sts before marker and k2tog. Repeat from * between the markers on back of hand (= 4 decreases per round).
Rnd 2: Knit around without decreasing.
Repeat Rnds 1 and 2 until 4 (6, 4, 4, 4) sts remain. Cut yarn and draw end through remaining sts; pull tight.

5 Thumb

Remove the contrast color yarn from the thumbhole. Pick up and knit 10 (10, 12, 12, 14) sts around the thumbhole. Knit 8 (9, 10, 12, 13) rnds. Next rnd: *K2tog, k1 (1, 2, 2, 3), k2tog*; repeat from * to * once more. Knit 1 rnd without decreasing. Next rnd: *K2tog, k0 (0, 1, 0, 1), k2tog*; repeat from * to * once more.
Next rnd: Sizes 5-6 and 7-9 yrs: *K1, k2tog. Sizes 10-12 yrs, women, men: *K2tog*; repeat from * to * around. Cut yarn and draw end through remaining sts; pull tight.
Weave in all ends neatly on WS.

Left Mitten

Work as for right mitten but place the thumbhole on the left side of the palm as follows: Slip 1st marker to the right needle, work until 4 (4, 5, 5,

6) sts remain before next marker, knit 4 (4, 5, 5, 6) sts with a smooth contrast color yarn; place the sts back on the left needle and knit again with pattern yarn. Complete as for right mitten.

Mittens with Doubled Cuffs

Worked as for the basic mittens after the ribbed cuff.

Casting on
With U.S. 10 / 6 mm dpn, CO 20 (20, 22, 24, 28) sts. Work around in stockinette for approx 2 (2, 2½, 2¾, 2¾) in / 5 (5, 6, 7, 7) cm. Turn piece inside out and work in stockinette for approx 2 (2, 2½, 2¾, 2¾) in / 5 (5, 6, 7, 7) cm.

Decorative Cords
Cut 3 equal-length strands of yarn (approx 80 in / 200 cm) long. Twist the strands together and cut cord in half. Tie a knot at each of the 4 ends. Securely sew the center of each cord below the foldline before sewing down facing.

Wrist Warmers

Wrist warmers can be knit as for the basic mitten until the piece measures approx 3¼ (3½, 4, 5¼, 6) in / 8 (9, 10, 13, 15) cm from ribbed cuff.
Top/finishing:
Work 2 (2, 3, 4, 5) rnds in k1, p1 rib. BO.
Thumb: Pick up and knit the appropriate number of sts and divide onto 4 dpn. Work in k1, p1 rib for 3 (3, 4, 5, 6) rnds and then BO. Weave in ends neatly on WS.

Mittens with Long Cuffs

Work as for the basic mittens after the end of the ribbed cuff.

Casting on: CO 20 (20, 22, 24, 28) sts and divide over 4 dpn; join, being careful not to twist cast-on row. Work around in stockinette for approx 2¾ (2¾, 3¼, 3½, 3½) in / 7 (7, 8, 9, 9) cm. Change color as desired. Work in k1, p1 rib for approx 2 (2, 2½, 2¾, 2¾) in /5 (5, 6, 7, 7) cm. Change to stockinette, increasing 0 (2, 2, 4, 4) sts evenly spaced on the first rnd = a total of 20 (22, 24, 28, 32) sts.

Flip-Top Mittens

Work as for the basic mittens up to the 1st decrease after the thumbhole.

1 Using a smooth contrast color yarn, knit the 10 (11, 12, 14) sts between the markers. Move the sts back to the left needle and knit again with pattern yarn. Knit 2 more rounds in stockinette.
2 Complete mitten with top shaping as for basic pattern.
3 Remove the contrast color yarn and divide the sts onto 2 dpn.
4 Lower needle: Work 2 rnds k1, p1 rib; purl 1 row and then BO.
5 Upper needle: Work 4 (5, 6, 8) rows stockinette and then 2 rows k1, p1 rib. BO.
6 Sew the sides of the top part down over the lower section. Weave in all ends neatly on WS.

Bags

The bags are knit in the round on U.S. size 10 / 6 mm needles. Knit your bag any size you like.
Yarn amount: 100 g.

The bags shown in the photos are worked as follows:
CO 60 (120) sts and join, being careful not to twist the cast-on row. Knit 4 (6) rnds in stockinette and then purl 1 rnd for the foldline. Continue in stockinette (working in a pattern if you like—the pattern is worked from the top down because the bag begins at the top edge). Work in stockinette for 7 (13½) in / 18 (34) cm. Now divide the sts evenly over 2 needles. Hold the needles parallel and, using a third needle, join the bottom of the bag with three-needle bind-off (see page 8).

Handles
There are several ways to make the handles—here are three:
1 Garter stitch handles
2 Doubled edge (stockinette)
3 Braided or twisted cords

Sew the handles securely to the inside of the bag. If the bag is lined, sew on the handles after sewing in the lining.

Garter Stitch
CO 60 (120) sts.
Work back and forth in garter st (knit all rows) for 2-2½ in / 5-6 cm and then BO. Make another handle the same way.

Doubled Edge (Stockinette)
CO 60 (120) sts.
Work 3 (4) rows back and forth in stockinette (knit on RS and purl on WS). Purl 1 row on RS (foldline). Knit 6 (8) rows, purl 1 row (foldline), work 3 (4) rows in stockinette. Fold the sides of the handle towards each other and seam. Make another handle the same way.

Twisted Cord
Cut 6 equal-length strands of yarn, approx 40 (80) in / 100 (200) cm long (use more or fewer strands depending on how thick or thin you want the cord).

Braided Cord

Cut 12 equal-length strands of yarn = approx 30 (60) in / 75 (150) cm. Braid the strands with 3 groups of 4.

Turn the bag inside out. Lay the bag on the lining fabric folded double. Cut out the lining around the bag, adding a ¾ in / 2 cm seam allowance.

If you want to make pockets for your bag, cut them out and sew them securely to the lining. Seam the lining along the sides and bottom.

Turn the lining right side out and pull it over the bag with wrong side out. Fold the knitted facing over the lining and sew it down securely with fine stitches.

RAGLAN SHAPING

Raglan shaping is a good choice for sweaters knit in the round, particularly when you want to make a sweater with some patterning but it is also effective for a single-color model. You knit the sweater as for any circularly-knit sweater up to the yoke. Instead of decreasing evenly spaced around the whole yoke, you decrease 8 sts on every other round, with the decreases falling on each side of the armhole all the way up to the neck.

KNITTING WITH BEADS

You can knit beads onto any garment and you can work them in with either circular or raglan shaping. Knitting beads on a garment is fun and makes it even more special.

Model 8

How to— Raglan Shaping

Follow the basic instructions for knitting in the round up to the yoke on pages 11 and 13.

After placing the sleeve and body sts on the same needle, place a marker (a safety pin will work) around both the last st of the sleeve and the first st of the body at each of the intersections between sleeve and body = a total of 4 places marked. Knit 1 rnd. On the next rnd, decrease with ssk before the marker, k2 (knit these 2 marked sts on all rnds), k2tog. Repeat the decreases at each marker = 8 sts decreased. Knit the next round without decreasing.

Move the markers up on every round. Continue alternating a knit round with a decrease round until 52 (56, 54, 58, 62) sts remain for child sizes. Dec 2 (6, 4, 6, 10) sts evenly spaced around on the next round. For adult sizes, decrease until 60 (58, 56, 66, 72) sts remain. On the next round, decrease 6 (4, 0, 8, 12) sts evenly spaced around. Work the neckband.

Chart for the Beaded Model

Child

108 (120, 126, 138, 150) sts

132 (144, 150, 162, 174) sts

156 (168, 174, 186, 198) sts

-8
-8
-8
-8
-8
-8
-8

Adult

-8 156 (162, 168, 186, 192) sts
-8
-8
-8 180 (186, 192, 210, 216) sts
-8
-8

204 (210, 216, 234, 240) sts

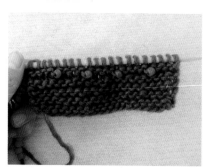

How to—Knitting with Beads

Loop the end of the yarn through a big-eye beading needle and string beads onto the yarn—40-50 beads should be enough. If you won't be knitting a section with the beads for a while, it is better to wait before stringing the beads. Just before you get to the place where you will knit in the beads, cut the yarn, string the beads, and splice the yarn. Begin the piece by casting on the number of stitches needed for the desired size of the garment/accessory.

There are two ways to knit in the beads. You can work in garter stitch (with ridges on both sides of the fabric) or stockinette (knit on RS and purl on WS), in which case you need to place the beads on a purl row on the RS. The beads lie on the strand between two stitches. When deciding how many stitches you want between beads, take into account the total number of stitches. If you are following the basic instructions for the sweaters in this book, you'll find that all the models that are charted are based on a multiple of 6 stitches. That means that you could place a bead at every 6th st.

Garter Stitch
On garter stitch fabrics, the beads are knitted in on the wrong side. Bring up a bead so it lies behind the right needle, knit 1 and pull the yarn to tighten. Knit to the next place for a bead.

Stockinette with a purl round
In this case, the beads will sit on the front of the work.
Purl and bring up a bead so it lies behind the right needle, purl 1 st and pull the yarn to tighten. Purl to the next place for a bead.

Model 10
Turquoise Model

Worked following the basic pattern (see pages 11 and 13) up to the yoke and then worked with raglan shaping (see page 59).

Body

With U.S. 10 / 6 mm circular, CO the specified number of stitches just above the lower edge (including the increases—for example, XS: 118 sts

+ 14 sts = 132 sts). Work in k1, p1 rib for ¾-1½ in / 2-4 cm and then in stockinette until piece measures 4 (4¾, 5½, 6¼, 7, 8, 8¾, 9½, 9¾, 10¼) in / 10 (12, 14, 16, 18, 20, 22, 24, 25, 26) cm. Change to U.S. 7 / 4.5 mm circular and work in k2, p2 rib for 2½ (2¾, 3¼, 3¼, 3½, 3½, 4, 4, 4, 4,) in / 6 (7, 8, 8, 9, 9, 10, 10, 10, 10) cm. Change back to U.S. 10 / 6 mm circular and work in stockinette for 6 (6¼, 6¾, 7, 7, 7½, 7½, 8, 8¼, 8¾) in / 15 (16, 17, 18, 18, 19, 19, 20, 21, 22) cm = a total of 12¼ (13¾, 15½, 16½, 17¾, 19, 20, 21¼, 22, 22¾) in / 31 (35, 39, 42, 45, 48, 51, 54, 56, 58) cm. Continue following basic instructions.

Sleeves

With U.S. 10 / 6 mm dpn, CO the specified number of stitches just above the lower edge (including the increases—for example, XS: 28 sts + 14 sts = 42 sts). Work in k1, p1 rib for ¾-1½ in / 2-4 cm and then in stockinette until piece measures 2 (2, 2, 2½, 2½, 2½, 2½, 2¾, 2¾, 2¾) in / 5 (5, 5, 6, 6, 6, 6, 7, 7, 7) cm. Change to U.S. 7 / 4.5 mm dpn and work in k2, p2 rib for 1¼ (1¼, 1¼, 1½, 1½, 1½, 1½, 2, 2) in / 3 (3, 3, 4, 4, 4, 4, 5, 5) cm. Change back to U.S. 10 / 6 mm dpn and stockinette, increasing 1 st each at beginning and end of the round. For child sizes increase on every 5th round; for women's, on every 6th round (see basic instructions for number of times to increase for each size).

White Model

Work following the basic pattern (see pages 11 and 13), raglan shaping (page 59), and the instructions for the cardigan with knitted-on buttonhole/button bands.

Body

Cast on as for the turquoise model but use color A for the lower part of the edging before changing to stockinette with white. After 4 rnds stockinette with white, work 3 purl rounds with beads, placing a bead between every 6th st and 5 rounds between each bead row. The number of beads per round depends on the garment size—for example, XS: a bead every 6th st for 204 sts = 34 beads.

Sleeves

Work as for the turquoise model but use color A for the ribbing on sleeve cuff and white for the remainder of sleeve. After 4 rnds in stockinette with white (above ribbing), purl 2 rounds with beads—place a bead between every 6th st and work 5 rounds between each bead round.

Yoke

Work as for the basic pattern but work 5 purl and bead rounds (or more bead rows on larger sizes)—place a bead between every 6th st and work 5 rounds between each bead round. See the chart on page 68.

White and Turquoise Cap

See pattern on page 46. With turquoise, CO the specified number of sts and work in stockinette for 3¼ (4¼) in / 8 (11) cm; change to white and follow the instructions up to 2 rnds after the last increase. Purl 1 rnd and knit in 23 (24) beads with 4 sts between each bead. Work in stockinette until piece measures 8 (10¼) in / 20 (26) cm. Knit 1 rnd with turquoise, purl 1 rnd and then knit 1 rnd. Change to MC and continue following the pattern.

Turquoise Cap

See pattern on page 46. After the last increase round, work 3 purl rounds with beads, with 5 rnds stockinette between each bead round. **Note:** So that there will be an equal number of stitches between each bead, place the beads after every 7th st.

Turquoise/White Bag

CO 60 sts with MC. Work in stockinette until piece measures 7 in / 18 cm. Divide work into 2 sections, place the back (30 sts) on a holder. Work on the front only: Purl 1 row on RS (foldline), work 4 rows back and forth in stockinette and the bind off. Work the back in stockinette with color A, stringing on 18 beads before attaching yarn. Work 4 rows stockinette and then begin decreasing on both sides on RS row. Purl back and then decrease again. Continue decreasing at each side of every RS row. When 6 sts remain, make a buttonhole and then decrease as set until 2 sts remain. The beads are worked into the pattern with 3 rows between each bead row—6 beads, 5 beads, 4 beads, 3 beads. The first bead row is worked when 24 sts remain: P2, bring up bead, p4, bring up bead, p4, bring up bead, p4, bring up bead, p4, bring up bead, p4, bring up bead, p2. Also see the description and chart for the bag on page 70.

Make the handles for this bag by twisting together 5 strands of yarn. For other options, see page 54. If you plan on lining the bag, read page 55 first. Sew on the handles securely before you sew in the lining.

Turquoise Bag

See instructions on pages 54 and 55. For this version of the bag, we knitted in 5 rows of beads on purl rows, with 5 sts between each bead. Work the first purl row with beads after the 6th rnd in stockinette and then work 6 rnds stockinette after each bead row.

See how to knit the doubled handles on page 54.

Model 11

These sweaters are worked following the basic instructions (pages 11 and 13) up to the yoke and finished with raglan shaping (see page 59).

Gray Model

Body: CO with MC, work ribbing at lower edge and then continue in stockinette with MC.

Sleeves: CO with MC, work ribbing for cuff; change to light gray and continue, following basic instructions, until sleeve is 8 (9½, 11, 11¾, 13) in / 20 (24, 28, 30, 33) cm long for child sizes and 14¼ (15, 15, 15¾, 15¾) in / 36 (38, 38, 40, 40) cm for women and 16¼ (17, 17, 17¾, 17¾) in / 41 (43, 43, 45, 45) cm for men. Change to MC.

Pink Model

Body: Work as for gray model.

Sleeves: With MC and U.S. 10 / 6 mm dpn, CO the number of stitches following the ribbing specified in the basic pattern (including the increased sts—for example, 5 years: 24 sts + 12 sts = 36 sts). Work in stockinette for ¾-1¼ in / 2-3 cm. Change to U.S. 7 / 4.5 dpn and work 3-5 rnds k2, p2 ribbing. Change to U.S. 10 / 6 mm needles and stockinette. Increase 1 st each at the beginning and end of the rnd on every 5th rnd for child sizes, every 6th rnd for women's and every 7th rnd for men's sizes (see basic instructions for number of times to increase for each size). Change to MC as for the gray model.

Scarf

Yarn amount: 200 g

This scarf is worked in garter stitch (knit all rows). String the beads before you start knitting. For this scarf we used a total of 108 beads or 54 beads at each end. With needles U.S. 10 / 6 mm, CO 160 sts (or desired number). Knit 2 rows and then work next row as follows: K3, *bring up bead, k6*; rep from * to * across until 6 beads have been knitted in. K94 (or until 33 sts remain), *bring up bead, k6*; rep from * to * until you've knitted in 6 beads and end k3. Knit back and then knit 1 more ridge (1 ridge = 2 knit rows). Next row: *K6, bring up bead*; rep from * to * until you've knitted in 6 beads; k88 (or until 36 sts remain); *bring up bead, k6*; rep from * to * until you've knitted in 6 beads, end with k6. Repeat the staggered bead row sequence until all the beads have been knitted in. End with 2 knit rows and then BO.

Model 12

Model 12

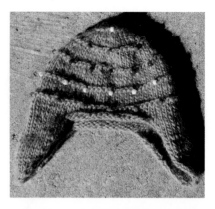

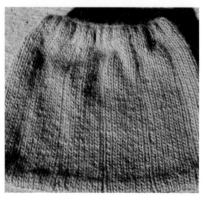

Hat with Earflaps

See basic instructions on page 46. Make the earflaps. String the desired number of beads on the yarn before you start knitting the hat in the round. The hat pictured here used 4 yellow, 8 red, 12 blue, 12 yellow, and 12 red beads. Work 3 rounds in stockinette, purl 1 rnd, knitting in the beads with 5 sts between each bead. Work 5 rnds stockinette between each bead row and shape hat as in the basic pattern.

Decorated Poncho

See chart. If you want to knit in beads as shown in the photo, string the beads before you start knitting. You'll need 26 (28, 29, 31, 33, 34, 35, 36, 39, 40) beads per row. Cast on the same number of stitches as when body and sleeves are joined: 5 yrs/156 sts, 7 yrs/168 sts, 9 yrs/174 sts, 10 yrs/186 sts, 12 yrs/198 sts, XS/204 sts, S/210 sts, M/216 sts, L/234 sts, XL/240 sts. Work a few rounds in ribbing or pattern of your choice for the lower edge. Knit in beads and shape as shown on the chart.

Neckband

Shape following instructions in the basic pattern on pages 11 and 13. Work in k2, p2 rib for 2-2½ in / 5-6 cm or in desired pattern. BO and then weave in ends neatly on WS.

Fringe

Attach fringe evenly spaced around the lower edge.

Muff

Begin by stringing beads onto the yarn. We used 45 beads for this muff: 5 yellow, 5 blue, 5 red, 5 yellow, 5 blue, 5 yellow, 5 red, 5 blue, and 5 yellow. CO 30 sts. Work 5 rows in stockinette. *Purl the next row on RS, placing beads after every 4th st (begin row with p4 and place bead). Work 5 rows in stockinette. Repeat from * until all the beads have been used. End with 5 rows stockinette. BO, cut yarn, leaving tail long enough for seaming. Graft the 2 long sides with mattress stitch. Make a cord by twisting 5 strands of yarn together.

Skirt

With circular U.S. 10 / 6 mm, CO 5 yrs/99 sts (7 and 9 yrs/108 sts, 10 and 12 yrs/117 sts, XS and S/126 sts, M and L/135 sts, XL/144 sts). Join, being careful not to twist cast-on row. Work around in stockinette for 1½-2½ in / 4-6 cm. Purl 1 rnd (foldline). Next rnd: *K8, p1*; rep * to * around. Continue as set, with knit over knit and purl over purl until skirt is desired length. Purl 1 rnd for the foldline. Work in stockinette for 1½-2½ in / 4-6 cm. BO and weave in ends neatly on WS. Fold under the facing at lower edge and sew down on WS with loose stitches. Fold down the facing at the top and sew down with loose stitches, leaving an opening for the elastic. If you want to line the skirt, sew in the lining first and then fold the facing over the lining and sew down. Insert elastic band through the casing and complete seaming.

Model 12

Child

52 (56, 58, 62, 66) sts

78 (84, 87, 93, 99) sts

104 (112) 116, 124, 132) sts

130 (140, 145, 155 165) sts

5 (7) yrs: begin here
156 (168) sts

9 (10) yrs: begin here
174 (186) sts

12 yrs: begin here
198 sts

Adult

68 (70, 72, 78, 80) sts

102 (105, 108, 117, 120) sts

136 (140, 144, 156, 160) sts

170 (175, 180, 195, 200) sts

XS (S): begin here
204 (210) sts

M (L): begin here
216 (234) sts

XL: begin here
240 sts

begin here

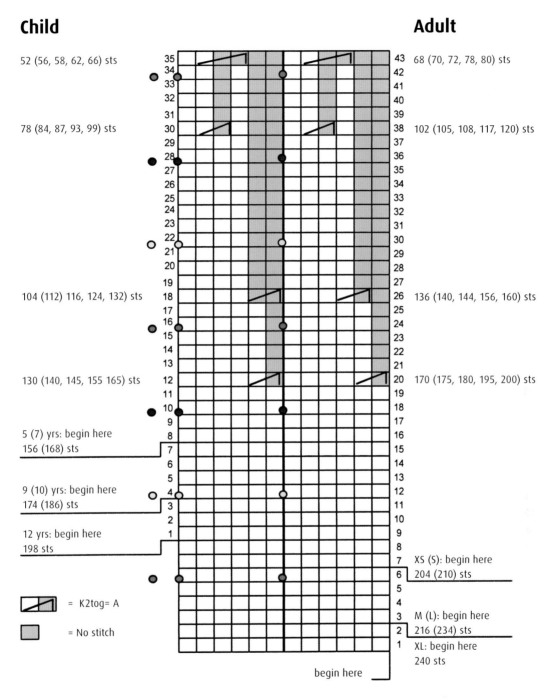

= K2tog= A

= No stitch

*Sweaters—see basic instructions,
pages 18 and 19*

Raglan shaping—see page 85

Models
13 and 14

The sweaters are worked following the basic sweater instructions on pages 11 and 13, with raglan shaping (page 59). The lower edge of the blue/white model is garter stitch (3 knit rows worked back and forth). The charted 4-row motif is worked before the raglan shaping begins. The beads are knitted in after every 6th st on every 6th round.

On the gray model, the lower edge is worked with 3 rounds MC, 2 rounds turquoise, 2 rounds MC, 2 rounds turquoise, and 4 rounds MC. The charted motif is then worked above the lower edge. Instead of beads, the yoke features a lice pattern with a contrast color on every 6th stitch on every 6th round. See chart.

Sweaters—basic instructions, pages 11 and 13. See page 59 for details about raglan shaping.

Child

108 (120, 126, 138, 150) sts

132 (144, 150, 162, 174) sts

156 (168, 174, 186, 198) sts

Chart for the Yoke 4

Adult

156 (162, 168, 186, 192) sts

180 (186, 192, 210, 216) sts

204 (210, 216, 234, 240) sts

⬛ = Main Color
⬛●

⬜ = On the blue/white model

◯ = Bead

Chart for Lower Edge

Beaded Bags

Bag

Yarn amount: 200 g
With U.S. 10 / 6 mm circular or dpn, CO 80 sts with dark gray; join, being careful not to twist cast-on row. Work around in stockinette until piece measures 9¾ in / 25 cm. Divide sts into 2 sets, placing the back 40 sts on a holder. Work the front as follows: Purl 1 row on RS (foldline). Work 4 rows back and forth in stockinette and then BO. Work the back/flap in garter stitch with light gray, stringing on 22 beads before you attach yarn. Work bead pattern following the chart, and, *at the same time*, decrease 1 st at each side on RS and then knit back. Continue decreasing 1 st at each side on every RS row until 4 sts remain. Make a buttonhole and then decrease as set until 2 sts remain. See chart. Seam bottom of bag.

Handles

With dark gray and U.S. 10 / 6 mm needles, CO 80 sts. Work in garter stitch for approx 2 in / 5 cm and then BO. For other handle options, see page 54. If you want to line the bag, see page 55. Sew on the handles before you sew in the lining.

Beaded Shawl

Yarn amount: 400 g
This shawl is knitted in garter stitch (knit all rows). With U.S. 10 / 6 mm needles, CO 2 sts. Work increases on RS rows as follows: Increase 1 st at the beginning and 1 st at the end of the row; knit back. Continue increasing the same way until there are a total of 66 sts.

BO the center 16 sts for a neck opening (see drawing below). Working only on the right side of the shawl, at neck edge, dec 1 st on every other row 3 times (for a rounded neck) = 22 sts. Continue in garter st until piece is 25½ in / 65 cm long or desired length. On the next RS row, dec 1 st at the beginning and 1 st at the end of the row; knit back. Continue decreasing the same way on every RS row until 2 sts remain and then BO. Work the left side of the scarf the same way.

The beads are knitted in on every 6th ridge with 4 sts between each bead. See chart.

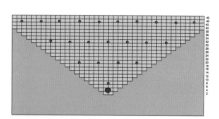

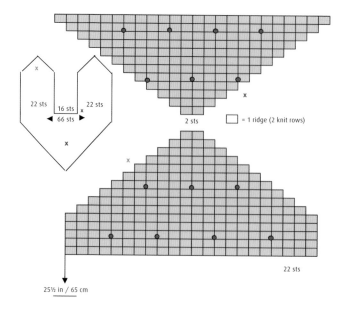

22 sts   16 sts   22 sts
◄ 66 sts ►

2 sts   ☐ = 1 ridge (2 knit rows)

22 sts

25½ in / 65 cm

Yarn Amounts for Raglan Models

	5 yrs	7 yrs	9 yrs	10 yrs	12 yrs	XS	S	M	L	XL
Model 8, 2 colors										
Main Color	4	5	6	6	6	7	8	8	9	9
A	1	1	1	1	1	1	1	1	1	1
Model 8, 1 color										
Main Color	4	5	6	6	6	7	8	8	9	9
Model 9										
Main Color	4	5	6	6	6	7	8	8	9	9
Model 10										
Main Color	4	5	6	6	6	7	8	8	9	9
A	1	1	1	1	1	1	1	1	1	1
Model 11										
Main Color	3	3	3	4	4	5	6	6	7	7
A	1	2	2	2	2	2	2	2	2	2
Model 12										
Main Color	4	5	6	6	6	7	8	8	9	9
Models 13 and 14										
Main Color	3	4	5	6	6	7	7	7	8	8
A	1	1	2	2	2	2	2	3	3	3
Model 15										
Main Color	4	5	6	6	6	7	8	8	9	9
A	1	1	1	1	1	1	1	1	1	1
Model 16										
Main Color	5	5	6	7	7	8	9	9	10	10
Model 17										
Main Color	5	5	6	7	7	8	9	9	10	10
A	1	1	1	1	1	1	1	1	1	1
B	1	1	1	1	1	1	1	1	1	1

PONCHO

If you can knit a scarf, you can knit a poncho! This poncho is constructed with two pieces that are sewn together. Here's a chance to use your imagination!

Moss stitch, garter stitch, beads, stripes, blocks, several colors, single color, etc, etc.

Models 16 and 17

Poncho Instructions

The length of the poncho depends on how many stitches you cast on. The large model shown in the photo started with 80 stitches. If you knit with U.S. 10 / 6 mm needles and have a gauge of 13 sts in 4 in / 10 cm, the width with 80 sts : 13 = 6.15 x 10 = 24¼ in / 61.5 cm. This will be the length from the neckline down to the wrist. The length of the poncho along the long side is determined by the size of the neck opening. Determine this length by measuring the short side against the long side and see how many lengths there should be for the desired size of the neck opening.

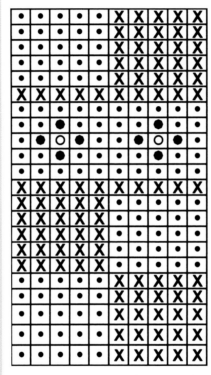

Chart for the vanilla white model

Neck Opening

Purple model: Work 1 rnd of single crochet around the neck.
Vanilla white model: Work 1 rnd of single crochet (sc) around the neck and then 1 rnd treble, and 1 round sc. Twist a cord with strands of yarn and thread through the treble crochet row.

●	= CC 2
○	= CC 1
•	= Knit
X	= Purl

Cap (see page 48)

Suggestions for Number of Stitches to Cast On

Fringes are made with 3 strands each.

Size	Cast on	Short Side	Long Side
5-7 yrs	40 sts	40 : 13 = 3.08 x 10 = 12 in / 30.8 cm	approx 24¾ in / 63 cm
9-10 yrs	50 sts	50 : 13 = 3.85 x 10 = 15¼ in / 38.5 cm	approx 28¾ in / 73 cm
12 yrs-XS	60 sts	60 : 13 = 4.62 x 10 = 18¼ in / 46.2 cm	approx 32¾ in / 83 cm
S-M	70 sts	70 : 13 = 5.38 x 10 = 21¼ in / 53.8 cm	approx 36¼ in / 92 cm
L-XL	80 sts	80 : 13 = 6.15 x 10 = 24¼ in / 61.5 cm	approx 40¼ in / 102 cm

1 Make two pieces the same size.

2-4 Sew the pieces together with the short side against the long side, using mattress stitch, back stitch, or knit them together by picking up 1 stitch from each piece and bringing the yarn through both stitches and binding off.

FELTING

Felting is one of the world's oldest fiber processing techniques. In the Nordic countries, you'll find written sources about felted garments in the Icelandic sagas. In the past, felting was done by hand. It was heavy and time-consuming work, with soft soap and water. This method is still used today and I have heard some say felting is very therapeutic. I call the felting method described here "cheating." The garments are knitted large and then felted in the washing machine. Nevertheless, the process is still very exciting. The garments are, as a rule, not recognizable after a round in the washer and they will be wonderfully warm.

General Instructions

Wash the garments to be felted in the machine with the water at about 104°F / 40°C. Use a little soft soap or Ivory—and pour the soap directly into the washer tub. The garments will shrink about 1½ in / 4 cm per 4 in / 10 cm in length and ⅜ in / 1 cm per 4 in / 10 cm in width (this can vary from washer to washer). Set the machine to a full washing program without a pre-wash (and not on the wool program). If you want to felt only one garment, we recommend adding a hand towel or something similar so that the garment has something to "work against." If the item is still too big after the first wash, wash it again at 140°F / 60°C. Stretch the garment to desired shape while it is still wet.

Yarn for Felting

For felting, I use 2 strands of Platu Lopi (unspun Icelandic pencil roving). Knitting with the 2 strands will be easier if you wind them together first. Pull up the innermost and outermost strands from the wheel and wind them together or use the innermost strands from two wheels to wind together.

Platu Lopi is a little tricky to knit with because it is unspun and can easily break. However, it is very easy to rejoin the ends. Overlap the ends by about 2 in / 5 cm and lightly roll them together between your palms. You can use the same technique to join on a new ball of yarn if the yarns are the same color.

Another yarn I recommend is Garnstudio's Eskimo which is 100% pure new wool that knits up at 10 sts and 14 rows = 4 x 4 in / 10 x 10 cm. The yardage of this yarn is 50 g = 54 yd / 50 m (CYCA #5).

Felted Hat

Sizes: 5-7 yrs (8-12 yrs, adult)
Yarn amount: 100 g
With U.S. 10 / 6 mm needles, CO 99 (108, 117) sts; join, being careful not to twist cast-on row. Work around in stockinette for approx 3¼ (3½, 4) in / 8 (9, 10) cm.
1st dec rnd: *K7, k2tog*; rep from * to * around = 88 (96, 104) sts remain.
Work in stockinette for approx 2 (2, 2½) in / 5 (5, 6) cm without decreasing.
2nd dec rnd: *K6, k2tog*; rep from * to * around = 77 (84, 91) sts remain.
Continue in stockinette for approx 6¼ (7, 8) in / 16 (18, 20) cm without decreasing.
3rd dec rnd: *K5, k2tog*; rep from * to * around = 66 (72, 78) sts remain.
Knit 5 rnds without decreasing.
4th dec rnd: *K4, k2tog*; rep from * to * around = 55 (60, 65) sts remain.
Knit 3 rnds without decreasing.
5th dec rnd: *K3, k2tog*; rep from

* to * around = 44 (48, 52) sts remain.
Knit 2 rnds without decreasing.
6th dec rnd: *K2, k2tog*; rep from * to * around = 33 (36, 39) sts remain.
Knit 1 rnd without decreasing.
7th dec rnd: *K1, k2tog*; rep from * to * around = 22 (24, 26) sts remain.
Knit 1 rnd without decreasing.
8th dec rnd: *K2tog*; rep from * to * around = 11 (12, 13) sts remain.

Cut yarn, draw end through remaining sts and pull tight. Weave in all ends neatly on WS.

Felted Cap

Sizes: 5-7 yrs (8-12 yrs, adult)
Yarn amount: 200 g
With U.S. 10 / 6 mm needles, CO 77 (84, 91) sts; join, being careful not to twist cast-on row.
Work around in stockinette for approx 10¼ (11¾, 13½) in / 26 (30, 34) cm.
1st dec rnd: *K5, k2tog*; rep from * to * around = 66 (72, 78) sts remain.
Knit 5 rnds without decreasing.
2nd dec rnd: *K4, k2tog*; rep from * to * around = 55 (60, 65) sts remain.
Knit 3 rnds without decreasing.
3rd dec rnd: *K3, k2tog*; rep from * to * around = 44 (48, 52) sts remain.
Knit 2 rnds without decreasing.
4th dec rnd: *K2, k2tog*; rep from * to * around = 33 (36, 39) sts remain.

Knit 1 rnds without decreasing.
5th dec rnd: *K1, k2tog*; rep from * to * around = 22 (24, 26) sts remain.
Knit 1 rnd without decreasing.
6th dec rnd: *K2tog*; rep from * to * around = 11 (12, 13) sts remain.
Cut yarn, draw end through remaining sts and pull tight. Weave in all ends neatly on WS.

Felted Stocking Cap

Sizes: 5-7 yrs (8-12 yrs, adult)
Yarn amount: 200 g
With U.S. 10 / 6 mm needles, CO

77 (84, 91) sts; join, being careful not to twist cast-on row.
Work around in stockinette for approx 6¼ (7, 8) in / 16 (18, 20) cm.
1st dec rnd: *K5, k2tog*; rep from * to * around = 66 (72, 78) sts remain.
Knit 6 (8, 10) rnds without decreasing.
2nd dec rnd: *K4, k2tog*; rep from * to * around = 55 (60, 65) sts remain.
Knit 6 (8, 10) rnds without decreasing.
3rd dec rnd: *K3, k2tog*; rep from * to * around = 44 (48, 52) sts remain.
Knit 6 (8, 10) rnds without decreasing.
4th dec rnd: *K2, k2tog*; rep from * to * around = 33 (36, 39) sts remain.
Knit 6 (8, 10) rnds without decreasing.
5th dec rnd: *K1, k2tog*; rep from * to * around = 22 (24, 26) sts remain.
Knit 6 (8, 10) rnds without decreasing.
6th dec rnd: *K2tog*; rep from * to * around = 11 (12, 13) sts remain.
Cut yarn, draw end through remaining sts and pull tight. Weave in all ends neatly on WS.

Felted Slippers 1-2-3

Make a slipper with a fun face. Knit, crochet, or sew ears, nose, and eyes.

We crocheted the ears for our slippers. For the eyes and nose, use glass beads. **Note:** Do *not* use beads on slippers for children younger than 5 years of age.

Sizes: 5-6 yrs (7-9, 10-12 yrs, adult)
Yarn amount: 100 g (100 g, 100 g, 200 g)

1 With U.S. 10 / 6 mm needles, CO 44 (48, 52, 56) sts. Work back and forth in garter stitch (knit all rows) until piece measures 7 (8¾, 10¼, 11¾) in / 18 (22, 26, 30) cm. BO 4 sts at each side.

2-3 Divide the sts evenly onto 4 dpn = 9 (10, 11, 12) sts on each needle. Work stockinette in the round for 3¼ (4¾, 6¼, 8) in / 8 (12, 16, 20) cm. Shape the toe with k2tog at the beginning of each needle on every round (= 4 dec per round) until 4 sts remain. Cut yarn and draw end through remaining 4 sts. Seam the opening at the back of the slipper. Weave in ends neatly on WS.

Felted Mittens—Basic Pattern

Sizes: 5 yrs (7-9 yrs, 10-12 yrs, women, men)
Yarn amount: 100 g

Right Mitten

With U.S. 10 / 6 mm dpn, CO 26 (30, 34, 36, 40) sts and divide evenly onto 4 dpn. Join, being careful not to twist cast-on row. Work around in stockinette until mitten measures approx 6¼ (6¾, 7, 8, 8¾) in / 16 (17, 18, 20, 22) cm.

Thumbhole

Place a marker on each side of the mitten, making sure there is the same number of sts on each side.
Knit the first 6 (6, 7, 7, 8) sts of the round with smooth contrast color yarn. Move the sts back to the left needle and knit again with pattern yarn. Continue knitting around for approx 4 (4¼, 4¾, 5½, 6¼) in / 10 (11, 12, 14, 16) cm after thumbhole.
Work the top of the mitten as follows:
Rnd 1: Sl 1, k1, psso (or ssk). Knit until 2 sts before marker and k2tog. Repeat these decreases between the markers (= 4 decreases per round).
Rnds 2-3: Knit 2 rnds without decreasing.
Repeat Rnds 1-3 until 6 (6, 6, 8, 8) sts remain. Cut yarn and draw end through remaining sts.

Thumb

Remove the contrast color yarn from the thumbhole. Pick up and knit a total of 14 (14, 16, 16, 18) sts around the thumbhole. Work 14 (15, 16, 18, 20) rnds in stockinette.
1st dec rnd: K2tog around = 7 (7, 8, 8, 9) sts remain.
Knit 2 rnds without decreasing.
2nd dec rnd: K2tog around until 4 (4, 4, 4, 5) sts remain.
Cut yarn and draw end through remaining sts. Weave in all ends neatly on WS.

Left Mitten

Work as for right mitten but place the thumbhole on the left side of the palm as follows:
Knit across until 6 (6, 7, 7, 8) sts remain before the marker on the left side; knit 6 (6, 7, 7, 8) sts with smooth contrast color yarn, place these sts back on the left needle and knit again with pattern yarn. Finish as for right mitten.

Felted Wrist Warmers

Make the wrist warmers as for the mittens (see basic pattern) until the piece measures approx 3¼ (3½, 4, 4¾, 5½) in / 8 (9, 10, 12, 14) cm above the thumbhole.

Finishing: Work in k1, p1 rib for 4 (4, 6, 6, 8) rnds and then BO.
Thumb: Pick up the specified number of sts for your size and divide sts onto 4 dpn. Work 4 (4, 6, 6, 8) rnds in k1, p1 rib and then BO.

Felted Flip-Top Mittens

Work as for the basic mittens up to the 1st decrease rnd after the thumbhole.

1 Using a smooth contrast color yarn, knit 13 (15, 17, 18, 20) sts between the markers. Move the sts back on left needle and knit again with pattern yarn. Knit 2 more rounds.
2 Shape top as for basic mitten pattern.
Finger opening:
3 Remove the contrast color yarn and divide the sts onto dpn.
4 Lower section: Work 4 rows k1, p1 rib and then BO.
5 Upper section: Work in stockinette for 8 (9, 10, 12, 14) rows; work 2 rows k1, p1 rib and then BO.
6 With top overlapping lower section, seam the sides of the lower and upper sections. Weave in all ends neatly on WS (also see instructions on page 74).

Felted Bags

Yarn amount: 100 g
The bags are knitted on a circular needle U.S. size 10 / 6 mm.
You can decide how big to make the bag. The bags shown here are worked as follows:

CO 80 (160) sts; join, being careful not to twist cast-on row. Work around in stockinette for 10¼ (16½) in / 26 (42) cm. Divide the sts evenly onto 2 needles. Hold the needles parallel and, using a third needle, work three-needle bind-off. Alternately, you can bind off all the stitches and then sew the bottom together. Weave in all ends neatly on WS.

Handles

These handles are knit in garter stitch. CO 80 (160) sts. Knit back and forth in garter st for approx 1½ (2) in / 4 (5) cm. BO and weave in ends on WS.
Sew the handles securely to the inside of the bag before it is felted.

Embellishment

For the bags shown here, we knitted 6 little patches in stockinette and then sewed a wooden button onto each patch. CO 5 (7) sts and work 5 (7) rows back and forth in stockinette. BO and weave in ends on WS.